Pearson's Canal Companion
FOUR COUNTIES

Published by J.M.Pearson & Son Ltd, Tatenhill Common, Staffordshire

Copyright: Michael Pearson - All rights reserved. Fifth edition 1995. ISBN 0 907864 68 6

Printed by Clifford Press of Coventry in association with the Portfolio Press of Barnoldswick

INTRODUCTION

FIVE editions breeds familiarity, but far from contempt, towards the FOUR COUNTIES RING. After all, this is the doyen of the Canal Companions. In its original manifestation, it was a simple - if not exactly naive - 48 page, 2 colour interpretation of the core circuit: no Caldon Canal, no Trent & Mersey south of Great Haywood, no frills. But, for all the limitations revealed by hindsight, it kick-started a career which has kept us clear of the Social Security register for thirteen years and spawned a series which now amounts to nine different titles covering the bulk of the inland waterways system.

It is still fun, though, to return, every three years or so, to the FOUR COUNTIES RING and its gentle, acquatic, peregrination of Staffordshire, Cheshire, Shropshire and the West Midlands, and to discover what changes have accrued on its 109 mile, 94 lock circuit. Half way through the Nineties, the route seems to be holding its own, remaining as popular as ever with boaters. The Caldon, however, continues to suffer from water supply problems which seem to keep it closed for lengthy periods each summer. It has also been fun to extend our coverage of the Trent & Mersey throughout from Preston Brook to Derwentmouth, reintroducing us to the strangely remote lowlands of South-east Derbyshire.

The greatest change to the presentation of this fifth edition, though, is the appearance, for the first time, of the maps in full colour. This has been an ambition of ours for many years, but hitherto costs have been prohibitive. Now, with the advent of desk-top publishing, we are looking forward to a new generation of Canal Companions printed in colour throughout with photographs, more or less in the appropriate position rather than being gathered, economically but disorientatingly, in one colour section. We hope you approve and thank you for your continued loyalty. Have fun!

Brewood

Wherever you see one of our boats - someone is having a marvellous holiday

We have 90 luxury narrowboats, with an average age of only 3 years, from 2-12 berths operating from 3 bases at Alvechurch, Anderton and Gayton offering a wide choice of canal and river cruising. Short breaks and 10/11 night holidays a speciality.

Write, 'phone or call in for a free colour brochure:
**Alvechurch Boat Centres, Scarfield Wharf, Alvechurch, Worcestershire B48 7SQ.
Tel: 0121-445-2909**

TRENT & MERSEY

EXTREMITIES: Main picture - Derwentmouth; inset - Dutton

PRESTON BROOK was one of the North-west's busiest canal junctions of yesteryear. It developed as an inland port where cargoes were transhipped between widebeam Mersey 'flats' and the narrowboats which plied the Trent & Mersey Canal. A substantial number of warehouses were erected to cater for this labour-intensive activity, which continued right up until the end of the Second World War. Indeed, narrowboats continued to trade to and from Preston Brook as late as the 1970s, following which the majority of the warehouses were demolished. The main survivor is the handsome flour warehouse near the northern end of the tunnel. The actual junction between the Trent & Mersey and Bridgewater canals lies a few yards inside the northern end of Preston Brook Tunnel. It isn't wide enough for narrow boats to pass inside, and access is controlled by a timetable at weekends. Neither is it exactly straight - being one of the earliest canal tunnels it seems that Brindley had yet to perfect the art of digging in a direct line. There is no towpath through the tunnel, so walkers must follow the old horse lane across the top, pausing perhaps to refresh the parts that boater's can't reach at the "Talbot Arms" in Dutton.

At the southern end of the tunnel the Trent & Mersey Company built a stop lock to protect their water supply from being drawn into the Bridgewater Canal. Nearby stands a drydock covered by a valanced canopy which has a distinct railway character. No surprise, for the dock was built by the North Staffordshire Railway, who owned the canal at one time, for the maintenance of steam tugs introduced in 1865 to haul boats through the tunnel in the absence of a towpath.

Between Dutton Lock and Bartington Wharf the canal traverses a luxuriant stretch of countryside. The glimpse of a ship gliding through Cheshire fields could be the highlight of your journey along this section of the Trent & Mersey Canal, for down in the valley runs the Weaver Navigation used, about twice a week, by sea-going vessels trading upstream as far as the chemical plants of Northwich.

Summary of Facilities

There's a post office store and pub close to the canal at PRESTON BROOK. You are spoilt for choice at BARTINGTON WHARF where three pubs are within easy reach of bridge 209. THE HORNS is well-reputed for its food; the LEIGH ARMS has nice stained glass window scenes of Weaver shipping; but to our mind the HOLLY BUSH, saved from oblivion by Burtonwood, is the most homely of the trio. Cross the Weaver, and you can patronise the RHEINGOLD RIVERSIDE INN. But, wherever you go, do take care of the A49's fast and furious traffic.

Boating Facilities

CLAYMOORE NAVIGATION - The Wharf, Preston Brook, Cheshire WA4 4BA Tel: 01928 717273. 4 to 10 berth hire craft and full boatyard facilities. Shop with gifts and provisions. BLACK PRINCE HOLIDAYS - Stoke Prior, Bromsgrove, Worcs B60 4LA. Tel: Bromsgrove 01527 575115. 4 to 10 berth hire craft from base by bridge 209, Acton Bridge. Boating facilities and shop on site - Tel: 01606 852945.

THE Trent & Mersey revels in its remarkably lovely journey through a rural landscape of rolling farmland interspersed with belts of deciduous woodland, eventually becoming engulfed in the dusky portals of Saltersford and Barnton tunnels. In common with Preston Brook they are just not wide enough to enable narrow boats to pass inside, but at 424 yards and 572 yards respectively, they are short enough to be negotiated without delay to oncoming traffic. A broad leafy pool separates the two tunnels and their old horse-paths continue to provide walkers with a connecting link across their tops.

Of all the so-called "Seven Wonders of the Waterways", the ANDERTON LIFT is arguably the most ingenious, and it is terribly sad that it has not performed its role of raising or lowering craft through the fifty feet disparity in level between the Trent & Mersey Canal and Weaver Navigation for a dozen years or more; though there are signs that some momentum towards its restoration is gathering. The lift was designed by Sir Edward Leader Williams, an eminent Victorian engineer and opened in 1875. A massive iron framework supported two water-filled caissons, each of which could carry a pair of narrowboats. Originally hydraulically operated by steam, early in the twentieth century it was converted to electrical operation using a system of counterbalance weights.

East of Anderton the Trent & Mersey winds around the outskirts of Northwich affording occasional glimpses of the town and its chemical industry nestling down in the valley of the Weaver. Centuries of salt production has destabilised the landscape. In 1958 a new length of canal had to be dug at Marston to by-pass a section troubled by subsidence. Lion Salt Works was the last in Britain still producing salt by the process of evaporation in open brine pans. By the mid Eighties it was struggling to compete with more up to date mass production techniques and finally went out of business. Now it is gradually being restored as a working museum. Rock salt was mined in much the same way as coal. One of the largest salt mines stood north-east of bridge 193.

Summary of Facilities

There are three pubs along this length; all offering food and catering for families. Alternatively, you could try THE MOORINGS, an informal, inexpensive eatery located at Anderton Marina. BARNTON has a a useful range of shops including chemist, butcher, baker, post office and Chinese take-away.

Boating Facilities

ALVECHURCH BOAT CENTRES - Scarfield Wharf, Alvechurch, Worcs B48 7SQ. Tel: 0121 445 2909. 2 to 12 berth hire craft. Full boatyard facilities at Anderton Marina (Tel: 01606 769642).

Map labels:
site of salt works 193
Spillers Foods
192
191
Original course of canal
Lion Salt Works
Wincham
Marbury Country Park
site of salt works
Marston
196
"The Moorings"
A.B.C.
Anderton
198
199
Weaver Navigation to Northwich & Winsford
70'
"Stanley Arms"
ANDERTON LIFT
200
ICI Winnington Works swing-bridge
Northwich town centre 1 mile
A533 to Runcorn
Barnton
70'
"Red Lion"
Little Leigh
204
Saltersford Tunnel
201
Barnton Tunnel
Saltersford Locks
205
206

Weaver Navigation to Weston Point

PREDOMINANTLY rural in character, the Trent & Mersey Canal makes its way through the peaceful valley of the River Dane, only the suburbs of Broken Cross and the ICI works at Lostock contrive to break the bucolic spell. The most curious feature of this section of the canal are the subsidence-induced flashes bordering the main channel to the south of bridge 181. That nearest the bridge was once filled with the submerged wrecks of abandoned narrowboats, an inland waterway equivalent of Scapa Flow. Many of the boats were brought here and sunk en masse during the Fifties in circumstances almost as controversial in canal terms as the scuttling of the German fleet at Scapa after the First World War. In what was probably a book-keeping exercise, British Waterways rid themselves of surplus narrowboats in a number of watery graves throughout the system. In recent years all the wrecks have been raised and taken off for restoration. One generation's cast-offs become the next's prized possessions. Hereabouts the Dane, nearing journey's end at Northwich where it joins the Weaver, has grown sluggish with age, meandering about its level valley in a succession of broad loops, so that at one moment it is hard by the canal, the next away across the fields of milking herds. The soil here is soft and the river carves deep banks shadowed by alder and willow.

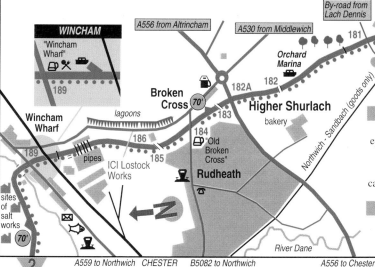

Summary of Facilities

Two attractive pubs punctuate your progress along this length of canal. The eponymous WINCHAM WHARF is a handsome warehouse conversion located alongside bridge 189. In contrast the OLD BROKEN CROSS is a long established, but recently refurbished, boatman's inn offering a good range of food. Fish & chips and Chinese take-away facilities are available close to the canal on the A559. The deeper in to RUDHEATH you go, the more shops, and a launderette, you'll find.

Boating Facilities

WINCHAM WHARF - Manchester Road, Lostock Gralam, Northwich CW9 7NT. Tel: 01606 48354. Pumpout, diesel, repairs, drydock etc; day boat hire.
ORCHARD MARINA - Rudheath, Northwich CW9 7RG. Tel: 01606 42084.

MIDDLEWICH is one of those towns which mean so much to canal travellers, but which motorists pass through without batting an eyelid. The suffix 'wych' is old English for salt and this key industry influenced the development of the Trent & Mersey Canal in many ways.

Five locks punctuate the canal's progress around the eastern edge of the town. The central three, deep and tediously slow to use, are bordered by compounds of stacked pallets and the uninspiring architecture of modern industrial units: all a far cry from the salty scenes of the past, when Seddon's and Cerebos were at their zenith and a forest of flaring chimney stacks supported the Middlewich sky. Seddons had a fleet of some dozen narrowboats. The *Sweden* has survived and we managed to photograph it at Shardlow.

CROXTON AQUEDUCT carries the canal over the River Dane not far from its confluence with the Wheelock. Originally the aqueduct was built to broad-beam dimensions. Close inspection of the undergrowth reveals some remnants of the old supporting piers. Now, ironically, it is just about the narrowest place between Middlewich and Preston Brook.

BIG LOCK lives up to its name. It recalls the original determination that the canal should be capable of taking widebeam craft inland from the Mersey ports as far as Middlewich. But then they skimped on the tunnels and the die was effectively cast.

Cruising through Middlewich on their research cruise, Les & Wendy came upon a trio of latter-day 'hobblers' happy to help them through the locks for the fun of it. Unlike their predecessors, however, they were versatile enough to be seen lock-working with the same degree of altruism at Audlem later in the week, bringing a whole new meaning to the term "lock-wheeling". Or perhaps they were simply a hush-hush government-sponsored pilot scheme for reducing the ranks of the unemployed. At Town Bridge Wharf a handsome, whitewashed warehouse is optimistically being advertised 'To Let' as a possible restaurant complex.

On the southern edge of town the Trent & Mersey Canal makes a busy junction with a branch of the Shropshire Union Canal, an important link in the Four Counties Ring circuit. The first few hundred yards of this branch, together with WARDLE LOCK, were actually built by the Trent & Mersey Canal Company. Nowadays boating can be hectic here as craft negotiate the tight turns into and out of the branch and the neighbouring KING'S LOCK.

Map labels:

chemical works

163 70' 162 161 5

Booth Lane Locks 28ft 9ins

164

165

Ah Bisto!

salt works

Rumps Lock 9ft 2ins

sanitaryware works

166

NEWS

Kings Lock 11ft 3ins

Middlewich Locks 32ft 7ins

A54 from Congleton

169

168

Key

🏭 Site of Seddons saltworks
🏛 Town Bridge Canal Wharf

Wardle Lock 9ft 9ins

Big Lock 5ft 0ins

70'

31

River Dane

A530 from Lostock Gralam

town centre

i

textile wrks.

70'

Middlewich

30

29

28

Croxton Hall

173

Middlewich Manor

mill

aqueducts

River Wheelock

DANGER 175

3

CROXTON AQUEDUCT

Stanthorne Lock 11ft 1in

27

39

A533 to Northwich

A530 to Nantwich

MIDDLEWICH (inset)

drydock

Kings Lock Chandlery

169

70'

Middlewich Narrowboats

168 167

Andersen Boats

31

Middlewich

A salt making town since Roman days, Middlewich has undergone much change in recent years as the traditional steaming pan method of manufacture has given way to modern vacuum techniques.

Eating & Drinking

BIG LOCK - canalside Big Lock. Handsome, Dutch-gabled redbrick pub overlooking eponymous lock. Much refurbished of late and now catering ambitiously with a wide variety of bar and restaurant dishes.
KINGS LOCK. Another pub named after a lock, this is a cosy little Tetley house. Outdoor table lock-side in summer.
Good fish & chip shop by Kings Lock.

Shopping

The shops of Middlewich are old-fashioned in an unselfconscious way and this is a pleasant spot to re-stock the galley. However, it says much for the age in which we live that Vernons once exquisite butchers has been turned into a video shop. There are NatWest and Barclays banks in Wheelock Street. There's a small market on Tuesdays whilst Wednesday is early closing day.

Public Transport

BUSES - frequent services to Crewe, Sandbach etc depart from the Bull Ring by the church. Tel: 01244 602666.

Boating Facilities

ANDERSEN BOATS - Wych House, Lewin Street, Middlewich CW10 9QB. Tel: 01606 833668. 4 to 10 berth hire craft (Hoseasons). Pumpout and gas.
MIDDLEWICH NARROWBOATS - Canal Terrace, Middlewich CW10 9BD. Tel: 01606 832460. 4 to 12 berth hire craft. Full range of boating facilities plus drydock, shop and laundry.
KINGS LOCK CHANDLERY - Booth Lane, Middlewich. Tel: 01606 737564. Moorings, gas, diesel, solid fuel, extensive chandlery and canal souvenirs.

Middlewich

L OCKS are abundant, and potentially habit-forming, as the Trent & Mersey ascends from (or descends to) the Cheshire Plain. There are twenty-six chambers to negotiate in only seven miles between Wheelock and Hardings Wood, and "Heartbreak Hill", as this section has been known to generations of boaters, seems an all too appropriate nickname by the time you have reached the top or bottom; 250 feet up or down. With the exception of the PIERPOINT pair, all the locks were 'duplicated' in the 1830s, both to speed up traffic in the face of railway competition, and to improve water usage by the use of inter-connecting paddles between adjoining chambers, enabling one lock to act as a mini-reservoir to its neighbour. These side-paddles were taken out of use when commercial traffic ceased towards the end of the 1960s, but the duplicated locks still ease delays today, as well as offering the opportunity to swap traveller's tales with boaters operating adjacent chambers.

The locks may, or may not, make life hard for the boater, but the canal itself is illuminated by a succession of small communities with interesting pasts. Sandbach stays a stubborn mile or more out of reach of the canaller, but you can enjoy the journey around its outskirts and intermittent views of the tower of its parish church. At ETTILY HEATH the quadrupled, electrified tracks of the Crewe to Manchester railway cross the canal at the site of an old transhipment basin which the Manchester & Birmingham Railway (one of George "The Railway King" Hudson's shady concerns) provided to facilitate traffic with the Potteries. Hereabouts the canal, concrete-banked and steel-piled, tends to be deeper than is usual on account of subsidence caused by salt-mining in the past. On either side of the canal flashes attract a variety of species of wildfowl and wading birds. The River Wheelock rises in the vicinity of Little Moreton Hall and gives its name to a former wharfingering community situated where the Crewe to Sandbach road crosses the canal. At one time no boatman worth his brine would be seen without a "Wheelock Windlass". MALKIN'S BANK was home to the families of boatmen engaged in comparatively short-haul traffics connected with the salt and chemical industries. They lived cheek-by-jowl with employees at the huge Brunner-Mond sodium carbonate works now buried beneath the greens and fairways of Congleton's municipal golf course. Between locks 62 and 63 a side bridge carries the towpath over an old arm which once went into the chemical works. At HASSALL GREEN the M6 motorway crosses the canal. Some of those lorries and cars will be in Stoke within quarter of an hour - you, dear boater, are a working day away!

Sandbach Railway Station

Ettily Heath

site of bone works

site of rail/canal transhipment basin

Yeowood Farm

River Wheelock

Sandbach 1 mile

site of salt works

Malkin's Bank

Wheelock Locks 79ft 6ins

M6 from The North

157   156   155   154   152

151

150

149

148

146   145

sewage works

66 65 dup dup

64 dup

63 dup

62

61 dup

60 dup   59 dup

58 dup

57 147

56   55

Wheelock

site of salt works

site of Brunner Mond chemical works

golf course

"Salt Line" ⓘ

Hassall Green

Pierpoint Locks 14ft 6ins

Pottery

chapel

A534 Crewe 5 miles

Locks marked 'dup' are duplicated - ie there are chambers side by side. you may use either chamber in either direction, but note that from time to time one chamber may be closed for maintenance.

M6 to The South   By-road to Alsager

Sandbach

Chiefly famous for its ancient Saxon crosses, Sandbach lies about a mile east of the canal at Ettily Heath, though there is easy access to the railway station from bridge 160. In transport circles Sandbach is lauded as the home of lorry making. Fodens had their roots in 19th century agricultural machinery and they were at the forefront of the development of steam lorries. Edwin Richard Foden (ERF) broke away from the family business to concentrate on diesel lorries and, seeing how successful he became, the family followed suit! You cannot drive very far nowadays without meeting a modern juggernaut built by one or other of these firms.

Wheelock

Useful spot for replenishing supplies before or after tackling the "Cheshire Locks". Three pubs provide plenty of choice. Canalside the CHESHIRE CHEESE serves Banks's and bar meals. Across the road the COMMERCIAL HOTEL is a real ale lovers' free house. Fish & chips and breakfast fry-ups from MRS B's. Shopping facilities include a general store, off-licence, newsagent and post office dealing in canalia. Frequent buses to Crewe and Sandbach.

Hassall Green

Just the place for a breather between lock flights. Surprisingly the M6 doesn't intrude and there are pleasant walks to be had along country lanes. Downhill, past the little mission church painted shocking pink, the old Sandbach branch of the North Staffordshire Railway has been converted into the "Salt Line" bridleway. There's a pottery adjacent to bridge 146 . Refreshments are available at the LOCKSIDE RESTAURANT, a homely cafe located above the canal shop or at the ROMPING DONKEY, a country pub only a few hundred yards north of bridge 147. The owners of the Lockside Restaurant also operate the post office stores which also stocks a good range of canal related material. Various boating facilities are also available here including pumpout, diesel and gas.

Wheelock

ONE hardly knows where to begin describing this richly rewarding and entertaining length of the Trent & Mersey Canal as it continues its passage through the long line of 'Cheshire Locks'. Again, all the locks were duplicated under the direction of Thomas Telford in the 1830s, though one or two have since been singled. Most peculiar of all, perhaps, was the rebuilding of one of the THURLWOOD LOCKS in 1958. Subsidence from the adjacent salt works had brought locks 53 to the brink of collapse, and so a new chamber was designed in the form of a steel tank supported by a series of piers which could be raised should further subsidence occur. Entry to the chamber was through guillotine gates. In practice the steel lock took longer to operate and was mistrusted by boatmen. It had been out of use for many years before demolition in 1987.

Another structure of significance was lost to the canalscape at RODE HEATH where a large warehouse with arched loading bay stood beside the canal until being controversially raised to the ground in 1981. Hearing that the mill, for long a local landmark, was to be demolished, the Trent & Mersey Canal Society succesfully applied to the Department of the Environment for the building to be listed as being of 'special historical and architectural interest'. In response the mill's owners took the matter up with their local MP, who must have had friends in high places for, just two months after being protected, the mill was de-listed. "After further consideration we came to the conclusion that the building was not as interesting as at first thought," quoted the DoE.

LAWTON 'TREBLE' LOCKS are Telford's work and replaced a Brindley staircase, both time-consuming and wasteful of water. At Hall's Lock the towpath changes sides. Beyond Church Locks there is a brief respite for the lockwheeler and the pleasant aspect of Lawton church at the edge of woods surrounding Lawton Hall. Throughout this length the countryside dips and sweeps away from the canal in folds and creases like a carelessly discarded garment; pastures interrupted by pockets of woodland through which footpaths beckon enticingly. Mow Cop (pronounced to rhyme with cow) overlooks this unspoilt landscape from its high ridge, an appropriate platform for the sober, yet lofty

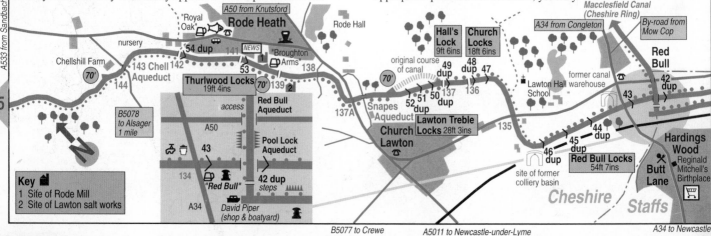

Key
1 Site of Rode Mill
2 Site of Lawton salt works

Red Bull

ambitions of the Primitive Methodists who held their first open air meeting on its summit in 1807. The castellated ruin, typical of 18th century romantic landscaping, is known as Wilbraham's Folly.

RED BULL LOCKS - once individually known as Townfield, Kent's and Yewtree in order of ascent - are probably the most visually satisfying on the whole of 'Heartbreak Hill'. All the elements are there by happy accident: a long, low stone wall separates the towpath from fields sloping down to the road edged by Lawton woods; the sweeping symmetries of the paired chambers masked from the railway by a high bank of beech trees; and an old whitewashed warehouse, once used for the storage of perishable goods.

POOL LOCK Aqueduct seems weighed down by the responsibility of carrying the Macclesfield Canal over the Trent & Mersey. It isn't by any stretch of the imagination an elegant work of engineering, but there's a doughty confidence in its demeanour, as if telling us it's stood here 150 years and good for a few more. Neither is the upper canal technically the 'Macclesfield', because it was the Trent & Mersey themselves who built the Hall Green Branch, the Macclesfield Canal proper beginning at Hall Green stop lock one mile to the north beyond a second bridge, the Red Bull aqueduct, which carries the canal over the A50 trunk road. The Macclesfield Canal is part of the popular "Cheshire Ring" canal circuit featured in another Pearson's Canal Companion and also recognised as a long distance footpath in its own right. Eastbound travellers along the Trent & Mersey, mystified by the Macclesfield's motive for crossing the T&M at this point, should turn to Map 7 for the exciting denouement.

Rode Heath & Thurlwood

Much expanded village at junction of A533 and A50. Two good pubs: the BROUGHTON ARMS, canalside by bridge 139, a well-appointed Marston's inn; and the ROYAL OAK (access from bridge 142) also comfortably furnished and well thought of for its food. There's a newsagent and off-licence by bridge 141 and a post office stores and butcher by bridge 139.

Red Bull & Butt Lane

Pleasant Robinsons pub overlooking lock 43 and interesting eating house up the A34 towards Butt Lane, a useful shopping suburb of Kidsgrove where Reginald Mitchell, designer of the Spitfire fighter plane was born.

Boating Facilities

DAVID PIPER - Red Bull Basin, Church Lawton, Stoke-on-Trent ST7 3AJ. Tel: 01782 784754. Pumpout, diesel, gas, moorings, repairs, boatbuilding etc; drydock and shop.

AT HARDINGS WOOD the Macclesfield Canal makes a junction with the Trent & Mersey. For eastbound travellers the mysteries of Map 6 are enlightened. If, on the other hand, you have just emerged, still blinking, from Harecastle Tunnel, you may be baffled to find a canal, destined for the north, making its exit to the south. All will be revealed on Map 6.

Taking a boat through Harecastle Tunnel is one of the inland waterway system's great adventures. At most times there is a tunnel keeper at either end responsible for controlling passage through the narrow bore. You may be delayed waiting for oncoming boats to clear the tunnel before the keeper gives you, and perhaps others going your way, instructions to enter. Gingerly you penetrate the gloom beyond the portal. Gradually all sense of light is lost. Nostalgically you look over your shoulder at the retreating half-moon of daylight. Suddenly, with a shuddering clang, the doors at the southern end close and the fume extractor fans begin to suck with a muted roar. For the next three-quarters of an hour you are under Harecastle Hill with one small niggle at the back of your mind. Will you, or won't you, come face to face with the Kidsgrove 'Boggart'?

The original tunnel through Harecastle Hill was designed by James Brindley. It took eleven years to build, was one and three-quarter miles long, and opened in 1777, five years after Brindley's death. A series of connecting tunnels led of the main bore to adjacent coal faces beneath Golden Hill, intersecting with several underground springs which provided additional water supplies to the summit level. A curious feature of this seepage occurs to this day, in that the water either side of the tunnel is tinted a peculiar orange shade by minute particles of ironstone rock. Stand on platform three at Kidsgrove station and you can witness something of the same phenomenon as similarly coloured water bubbles up from beneath the sleepers.

For fifty years, teams of 'leggers' propelled boats through Brindley's towpathless tunnel, lying on their backs at right angles to the boat and literally 'walking' from one end to another, a feat which took two to three hours depending on the amount of alcohol consumed beforehand. Not surprisingly Harecastle became a serious traffic bottleneck. Reluctantly, being well aware of the costs and difficulties involved, the canal company commissioned a second bore with Thomas Telford as consultant engineer. Some idea of the advances in technology gained in the interim can be gauged from learning that the new tunnel, equipped with a towpath, was completed in less than three years, opening in 1827.

Until the early years of the 20th century, the two tunnels were used in unison: Brindley's taking

HARDINGS WOOD & KIDSGROVE

Gas, diesel, solid fuel

41 dup

T & M

98

132

Access to Kidsgrove Town Centre

"Macc"

HARDINGS WOOD JUNCTION

131

Tunnel Keeper

Kidsgrove

4 Counties

Town Centre

Kidswood

132

98 dup

131

97

Harecastle Tunnel North Portal

airshaft

Boathorse Road

airshaft

Ravenscliffe

Traveller's Camp

Tunnel Keeper

130

70'

Harecastle Tunnel South Portal

site of Goldendale & Ravensdale Ironworks

site of Ravensdale Forge

site of Chatterley coal & iron works

By-road from Tunstall

128

129

Westport Lake

P

127

LONGPORT

Longport Marina

pottery

126

"Pack-horse"

NEWS

"Duke of Bridgewater"

"Railway"

A527 from Tunstall | B5051 from Burslem

70'

126

Longport

STOKE

A527 to Newcastle-under-Lyme

southbound boats, Telford's north. In 1914 electric tugs began to haul strings of boats through Telford's tunnel and Brindley's, now riddled with subsidence, was abandoned. The tugs were curious machines, unique on our waterways. They dragged themselves along a steel cable laid on the canal bed, collecting power through a tram-like pole from an overhead cable. They successfully solved Harecastle's traffic flow problems into the 1950s, by which time the number of boats using the tunnel had diminished so as to render them unviable. In 1954 forced ventilation was introduced, enabling powered boats to pass through, a system still in use today. Further subsidence caused closure of the tunnel between 1973-77, but much money has been spent on its rehabilitation in recent years, so it is now in excellent condition, and sporting a brand new keeper's office at the Kidsgrove end. And the Boggart? Well every canal tunnel seems to have a ghost - some even run to amphibious cows - but every now and then the tunnel keepers come across an apparent discrepancy in the number of boats entering the tunnel at one end and emerging at the other!

Refurbishment of the tunnel involved removal of the towpath, so walkers are faced with the option of catching a local train between Kidsgrove and Longport, or following the old boathorse route across the top, encountering the arcane, unvisited landscape of Harecastle Hill which Brindley and Telford must have been familiar with in their time. It seems little changed, and the chattering magpies which keep you company may quite possibly be re-incarnated navvies. Nearing the hilltop, the lane becomes more potholed, bounded with rough pasture grazed by unkempt ponies. Airshafts trace the tunnel's subterranean passage, whilst at its remotest the lane is straddled by a traveller's encampment. Breathtaking views encompass Jodrell Bank, the Wedgwood monument and the residually smoky panorama of The Potteries. In fact, all things considered, this is an adventure every bit as exciting as the boater's rite of passage underground. Heads or tails?

Between Harecastle's southern portal and LONGPORT, the canal runs along its 408ft summit at the foot of a ridge supporting Tunstall, northernmost of the six Potteries towns. Industry once thronged the cut, but there is an air of desolation here now. From bridge 129 to 130 the vast Ravensdale ironworks framed the canal, as massive in its heyday as Shelton Bar, three miles to the south. Today, though, no trace remains at all, and youths with air rifles and impassive anglers seem to be the only inhabitants of this wasteland. For the industrial archaeologist, however, the adrenalin will be flowing. Look out for Copp Lane canal cottages by bridge 129, the ruined edge of the side bridge which spanned the ironworks arm, and the stubs of old basins where the gasworks stood by bridge 128.

When Potteries folk haven't enough in their piggy banks to cover the fare to Blackpool or Rhyl, they come down for the day to WESTPORT LAKE where they can indulge in a ninety-nine and promenade the circumference of the lake, re-opened after its landscaping by no less a personality than the former Prime Minister, Edward Heath. The lake provides an amenity for itinerant and insolvent boaters too, providing pleasant overnight moorings, usually with the sense of security engendered by the proximity of fellow travellers.

In the vicinity of LONGPORT some of the traditional aspects of North Staffordshire make their presence felt. A fine example of the once ubiquitous bottle kilns looms over the canal by the premises of Price & Kensington, whilst, by Middleport Pottery, a series of old cranes hang over the water's edge as if the arrival of the next narrowboat laden with felspar or flint is imminent. Longport Wharf itself remains intact, a typical canalside depot where consignments would be collected and delivered by road transport, or perhaps warehoused for the benefit of the consignee.

Longport

Refer to page 71 for details of HARECASTLE TUNNEL operating timetable. Lock 41 is duplicated: either chamber may be used in either direction.

Kidsgrove

A former colliery town on the wrong side of Harecastle Hill to qualify as a member of that exclusive hell fire club called The Potteries. Its initially foreboding air thaws on closer acquaintance. A path leads up from the tunnel mouth to St Thomas's "the bargee's church" and there are waymarked ways through nearby "Kidswood". James Brindley is buried at Newchapel, a couple of miles to the east.

Eating & Drinking

Even the "Good Beer Guide", usually a champion of 'spit & sawdust' establishments, cannot muster a single public house of note in the town, though from time to time we get favourable reports of THE BLUEBELL by lock 41. Nearer the town centre THE HARECASTLE advertises Burtonwood ales, food and that it caters for families.

Shopping

Kiddy's shops are its strongpoint. They may look dour from the street, but inside the locals are at their most vital and receptive to visitors. London Road misleads you into thinking that there is nothing more. But duck under the old 'Loop Line' railway bridge - which no-one has ever bothered to remove - and you'll discover the real heart of the town and a small market on Tuesdays. Gravitate to BRENDA'S where you can watch oatcakes and pikelets, those twin bastions of Potteries gastronomy, being freshly made on the griddle, and have your oatcakes crammed with a choice of fillings. More mundanely, there is a KwikSave supermarket and branches of NatWest, Barclays and TSB banks. Calor gas and solid fuel from SMITHSONS by bridge 132.

Public Transport

BUSES - Potteries Motor Traction may well invoke quite different physiological emotions in female minds, but they provide an excellent service throughout the region. Tel: 01782 747000.
TRAINS - hourly service to/from Longport and Stoke. Tel: 01782 411411.

Longport

All the 'ports' - Long, Middle, West and New - lie down in the valley beside the canal and the origin of their names is obvious, forming as they do, a necklace of wharfingering communities where the import and export of cargoes of The Potteries were dealt with. Longport, lying as it does on a busy link road with the A500, makes few concessions in appearance. Lorries thunder through it leaving a tidemark halfway up the fronts of shops where merchandising and point of sales are unheard of phenomenons. Inside, bare counters display the meagre stocks which constitute essentials. Brand names that have disappeared from more sophisticated shelves eke out a twilight of diminishing trade for their manufacturers. Sweets still come in jars, sausages in links, vegetables in brown paper bags, and service with a penetrating smile of sincerity.

Eating & Drinking

THE PACKHORSE - canalside bridge 126. Ansells. Food. Karaoke on Saturday nights!
DUKE OF BRIDGEWATER - canalside bridge 126. Bass. Food.
Fish & chips either side of bridge 126. Sandwich shop dispensing Wrights pies.

Shopping

Selection of small shops placed conveniently either side of bridge 126 with mooring easy. Tea pots 'hot from the kiln' at Price's factory shop. Secondhand bookshop opposite open Wed-Sat.

Public Transport

BUSES - 10 minute frequency PMT services to/from Newcastle (good shopping) and Burslem.
TRAINS - refer to Kidsgrove.

Boating Facilities

LONGPORT MARINA - Longport, Stoke-on-Trent ST6 4NA. Tel: 01782 813831. Diesel & gas, servicing & repairs, boatbuilding (STOKE-ON-TRENT-BOATBUILDING) gritblasting, sales & brokerage and chandlery.

Middleport

THE Trent & Mersey Canal plunges through the heart of the manufacturing district it was built primarily to serve. It is a heart, however, broken repeatedly as heavy industry has given way to the microchip. Until 1978 the canal penetrated the torrid core of Shelton Bar steelworks, scene of H.G.Wells' terrifying short story, "The Cone", in which the steelmaster murders his wife's would-be lover by pushing him into a furnace. Nowadays only a rolling mill, supplied with steel blooms brought in by rail from Teeside, remains in use, though canal travellers are still required to pass through the gloom of two overhanging fabrication sheds. The derelict acres left behind after demolition of the blast furnaces became the site of the 1986 National Garden Festival, subsequently developed into the Festival Park, a mix of leisure, retail and commercial facilities. Such transformations are not without irony. Centrepiece of Festival Park is a hotel converted from Josiah Wedgwood's original Etruria Hall built on a green-field site contemporary with construction of the canal. During the 19th century the steelworks had encroached on the mansion, gradually engulfing its landscaped grounds. So, in a way, the developments of the 1980s returned the neighbourhood to its origins. Though anyone familiar with the canal prior to the shutdown of Shelton Bar is bound to mourn the lost drama associated with the taking of a boat through the cacophonous and acrid plant.

Like all the other once heavily industrialised regions of The North, The Potteries have passed through a period of transition; though here, perhaps, the pace of change has been less relentless, and something of the old atmosphere is still very tangible. From time to time you come upon examples of the area's most potent symbol, the bottle kiln. There was a time, before the Clean Air Act, when visitors could purchase postcards depicting The Potteries' skyline blackened by the combined emissions from serried rank upon rank of these ovens.

Etruria

For reasons never convincingly explained, Arnold Bennett - who is to The Potteries as Hardy to Wessex or Lawrence to Nottinghamshire - always referred to just 'Five Towns' in his prolific novels and short stories which portray the area around the turn of the century. He once wrote that the Five Towns could never be described adequately because Dante had lived too soon. Inferno or not, five towns or six, there was always, and still to some extent is, a proud independence and individualism about The Potteries which sets it apart in an island between the Midlands and the North. Notice how the local accent has more in common with Merseyside than Manchester: could this have something to do with the development of the Trent & Mersey and the associations it prospered? Between MIDDLEPORT and ETRURIA the canal twists and turns frequently, following the contours of the valley of the Fowlea Brook. Near bridge 125 stands the terracotta gabled end of the Anderton Boat Company's former premises, a well known canal carrier in the district whose boats were nicknamed "The Knobsticks". By bridge 123 an arm once led to Burslem Wharf, scene of the pantechnicon's immersion in Bennett's hilarious novel, "The Card". The arm was abandoned in 1961 after a breach caused by subsidence. Diesels shunt steel around the purlieus of Shelton works whilst varying degrees of skill are displayed on the ski slope opposite. A steel girder bridge is still in place where the old 'Loop Line' railway weaved its way from one Six Towns community to the next. A wooden, windlass-operated lift bridge frames entry to the Festival Park Marina. Secure moorings are available here for an overnight stop. Opposite are the premises of the "Evening Sentinel", Stoke-on-Trent's evening newspaper. This was the original site of the Wedgwood Pottery before subsidence and pollution forced the company to move to Barlaston. All that remains of the pottery is an enigmatic roundhouse, one of two which fronted the works. The canal once widened considerably at this point, and an arm reached round to the western side of the works. ETRURIA JUNCTION has all the ingredients of a compelling canalscape and ought to find a niche in most enthusiasts' 'Alternative Seven Wonders of the Waterways', along with such acquired taste locations as Wigan Pier, Trent Falls and Windmill End. One grieves, though, the loss of the roof which formerly spanned the top lock, similar in style to that at Barbridge Junction (Map 38). Much of Etruria's surviving charm emanates from the juxtaposition of the two top locks of the Stoke Five and the handsomely constructed and resonantly named Etruscan Bone Mill lying beside a small arm issuing from the tail of the second lock down. This now houses the Etruria Industrial Museum. Also of interest is the old graving dock, an intriguing milepost to Uttoxeter, a statue of Brindley, and the proximity of the deep staircase locks at the start of the Caldon Canal: all good stuff for the diehard to get their teeth into. Etruria's busy basin lay on the outside of the sharp bend at the commencement of the Caldon Canal. It did not always deal solely in commodities. In the 1840s, during a time of depression for the

FESTIVAL PARK & ETRURIA

Retail Park
"Rose & Crown"
Bedford Street Staircase Locks
Entertainment Centre
Brindley Statue
Caldon Canal
City Centre
Festival Park Marina
A53
Forge
"China Garden"
Black Prince
Etruria Industrial Museum
T & M
117
116
70'
"The Sentinel"
NEWS
Middleport 70'
Crse of Burslem Arm
park
123
125
7
Festival Park
119
Shelton Steel Works
A53
3
118
ETRURIA JUNCTION
4 Counties
Asda
Wolstanton
Etruria
A500
A53 to Newcastle-under-Lyme

Caldon Canal to Leek & Froghall continued on Map 41
A5009 from Leek
10
a b c d
9
8
6
Hanley
Hanley Park
College
Planet Lock 3ft 10ins
Bedford Street Locks 19ft 3ins
site of Etruria Basin
2
40
5
115
cemetery
5
3
4
Stoke Locks 40-36 50 feet
Trent Aqueduct
113
70'
Civic Hall
Town Centre
Victoria Ground
Stoke
36
110
8
Dolphin
111
7
9 wagon works
Course of Newcastle Canal
Mount Pleasant
Fenton

Key
1 Middleport Pottery
2 Former Mersey & Newport Potteries
3 Site of Wedgwood Pottery
4 Cliffe Vale Pottery
5 Former flour mill
6 English China clays
7 Former North Staffs Railway Works
8 Colonial Pottery
9 Site of Kerr Stuart locomotive works
a Hanley Pottery (disused)
b Eastwood Pottery
c Imperial Pottery
d Anderton Boat Co
e Port Vale Mill

A53 to Newcastle-under-Lyme

*Figures refer to Trent & Mersey, allow 1 hour for Caldon Canal

pottery trade, large numbers of emigrants began a long, life-changing journey aboard narrow boats from this wharf, destined for Wisconsin in North America, where a township called Pottersville was established.

Southwards from Etruria, the Trent & Mersey negotiates STOKE LOCKS, a fascinating flight, brim-full of images jostling for your attention: a ruined flour mill by the third lock down; a cemetery providing a splash of green in a sea of otherwise grey industry; a pair of colourfully painted railway bridges (one carrying a branch into English China Clays' works which receives this commodity in rail tankers now, whereas once it would have been brought round the coast from Cornwall to the Mersey and transhipped into narrowboats for the journey down to The Potteries) and the bottom lock in the flight, deep and concrete lined, a rebuilding dating from construction of the adjoining Queensway.

By bridge 113, the NEWCASTLE-UNDER-LYME Canal once diverged from the main line. opened in 1798, it ran in a V shape for 4 miles to the nearby borough of that name which, curiously, already had a canal. The Sir Nigel Gresley Canal, a 3 mile private waterway unconnected with any other canals, had opened in 1775 to carry coal from outlying collieries belonging to the Gresley family into Newcastle itself. The Newcastle Junction Canal was subsequently built to link the two canals, but an inclined plane, planned to bridge the disparity in height between the two 'Newcastle' canals was never built. Not surprisingly, all three canals were early casualties of the Railway Age. Stoke Boat Club used the first few hundred yards of the canal as moorings in the Sixties, but all trace of the entrance vanished with construction of the adjacent dual carriageway.

Road and railway escort the canal out of Stoke like two hefty nightclub bouncers ejecting a customer who has failed the sartorial test. But the Trent & Mersey preserves its dignity, crossing the tiny Trent, passing a boatyard, and heading out into open county beneath the new A50 link road and past the city's refuse incinerator. Our map shows the site of Kerr Stuart's locomotive works where L.T.C. Rolt served an apprenticeship for three years from 1928. He writes as vividly as always about his days in Stoke in "Landscape With Machines", his first volume of autobiography. Stirring tales of another sort are inseparable from the history of the Victoria Ground on the opposite bank of the canal, the home of Stoke City Football Club. Many famous players have worn the red and white stripes of the 'Potters' - one remembers with affection the early Seventies team of Dobing, Eastham,

Hudson, Greenoff, Pejic, Smith, Shilton and Mahoney - but most heroic of them all was Stanley Matthews, who last played for the club on 6th February 1965 at the astonishing age of 50. Thirty years later, he confessed at celebrations to mark his eightieth birthday, that he had felt that he still had a couple of more years in him when he retired.

The Caldon Canal

The inland navigator, setting off from Etruria on the thirty mile trip to Uttoxeter, inferred by the milepost at the junction, is in for a disappointment. They can travel for seventeen miles to the remote wharf at Froghall, hidden deep in the woodlands of the Churnet Valley, but the canal onwards from that point to Uttoxeter itself was filled in and converted into a railway a century and a half ago. Nevertheless, the Caldon is one of the most delightful waterways in England, a thing of rare beauty, all the more enchanting because it is under-utilised, being unfathomably ignored by the majority of hire-boaters; though perhaps this only adds to its appeal.

From Etruria the Caldon Canal immediately declares its intentions, ascending a deep pair of staircase locks, followed by another single lock as it skirts Hanley, chief of the Six Towns. Dipping through an overbridge, it runs beside a stone wall over which peeps a typical northern terrace. This simple throw-back explains eloquently enough the inherent pathos of The Potteries: backyards with rain-water tubs and washing-lines; cobbled alleyways patrolled by stray dogs; net curtains blown softly by draughts unhampered by double-glazing. In another place, not far to the North, you would immediately think of Lowry or Coronation Street. But these are The Potteries, as warming, full of flavour, and unsusceptible to the march of time as a Wrights steak & kidney pie.

PLANET LOCK - put in during the Twenties to solve water-level problems brought about by subsidence - is the most suitable point to moor for a short visit to Hanley. Twisting past more terraces, the canal bisects Hanley Park, passing beneath a series of ornamental bridges. From a balcony embellished with terracotta, steps climb to a clock-towered pavilion from which you half expect Arnold Bennett characters to emerge at any moment. Then a corridor of pottery works is encountered, though sadly no longer served by specially built craft carrying crokery from one department to another.

Continued on Map 41, page 65.

Hanley

Arnold Bennett, his tongue perhaps not entirely in his cheek, called his 'Hanbridge' the Chicago of the Five Towns, which was his way of clarifying the confusing situation whereby it is in Hanley that one encounters the commercial heart of Stoke-on-Trent, and not in Stoke itself, which is just one of the six communities along with Tunstall, Burslem, Hanley itself, Longton and Fenton which were merged to form Britain's fourteenth largest city in 1910. In any case, the people of The Potteries have never been particularly enamoured at the prospect of belonging to an amorphous whole, preferring to shelter within the proudly individual characters of the six constituent towns. Hanley has suffered most from the pressures of the Consumer Age, and development has exorcised a good deal of the previously entrenched atmosphere of dignified northern provincialism.

Eating & Drinking

One senses that 'eating-out' is not an activity buried deep in The Potteries psyche. Consequently there is a dearth of restaurants and eating places of the kind you would expect a city centre to provide. Wanting to take her Burslem-born mother out for a 'nice' afternoon tea, a friend asked the Tourist Information Centre to for a recommendation and was directed to Whitmore, 5 miles west of Newcastle! But at least Etruria catters for a passing trade of sorts:
CHINA GARDEN - canalside Festival Park. Plush new pub built for the Garden Festival. Seems a bit out on a limb now, but offers boaters a welcome chance to eat out inexpensively with their families.
ROSE & CROWN - adjacent bridge 118 (see enlargement). Traditional street corner pub overshadowed by A53 flyover but unspoilt within. Burton Ale and guest beers; bar and restaurant meals. Nice etched windows recalling Parkers Brewery. Several 'restaurants' are contained within the Festival Park complex including: PIZZA HUT, FATTY ARBUCKLE'S AMERICAN DINER and MCDONALDS.

Shopping

All facilities are available in the centre of Hanley which is about 20 minutes walk from the Trent & Mersey at Etruria, but less distant from the Caldon at bridges 4 or 8. Frequent PMT buses run from stops on bridge 118. THE POTTERIES CENTRE houses all the usual chain stores. We prefer the MARKET HALL, an atmospheric showcase for local retailing. North Staffordshire delicacies include 'oatcakes' and 'pikelets'; whilst Wrights have a number of outlets specialising in their tasty meat pies which differ from most of their mass produced competitors by actually including a fair proportion of real meat. Despite its uncouth image, Hanley is also well endowed with bookshops, both new and antiquarian, most of which stock an interesting selection of local tiltes. Numerous pottery works throughout the area have their own factory shops. An hourly bus service operates from Stoke station connecting with many of these premises. Full details of these can be had from the Tourist Information Centre. There is also a retail area at Festival Park dominated by a huge Morrisons supermarket.

Places to Visit

TOURIST INFORMATION CENTRE - Quadrant Road, Hanley ST1 1RZ. Tel: 01782 284600.
CITY MUSEUM & ART GALLERY - Bethesda Street, Hanley. Tel: 01782 202173. Open daily, admission free. A superb museum which puts those of many larger cities to shame. Predictably fine collection of ceramics, a section devoted to local man Reginald Mitchell's Spitfire fighte rplane, but not as much as there ought to be about Arnold Bennett.
ETRURIA INDUSTRIAL MUSEUM - canalside bridge 116. Open Wed-Sun 1am-4pm. Tel: 01782 287557. Restored potters mill of exceptional interest look after with obvious relish by a small band of devotees. The mill dates from 1857 and was built to grind animal bones for use in 'bone' china. Shirley's, the original owners, are still in business in more modern premises nearby. Beam engine steamed monthly.

FESTIVAL PARK - Etruria. Access from canal via bridge 118. Attractions include: multi-screen cinema (Tel: 01782 215311); Waterworld swimming centre (283838); dry ski slope (204159); bowling rink; snooker club; Quasar laser centre etc.

Public Transport

BUSES - PMT services throughout The Potteries. Tel: 01782 747000. Local services display such evocative destination blinds as "Brown Edge" , "Fegg Hayes" and "Talke Pits".

Boating Facilities

BLACK PRINCE HOLIDAYS - Stoke Prior, Bromsgrove, B60 4LA. Tel: 01527 575115. 2 to 10 berth hire craft based at Festival Park Marina.
MARINE SERVICES (Tel: 01782 201981) location as above. Full range of boatyard facilities plus gift shop.

Stoke

Known as 'Knype' in Arnold Bennett's stories, Stoke was, and still is, the railhead for The Potteries. Here, his Five Towns characters waited for the old Loop Line trains to take them to 'Hanbridge' (Hanley), 'Bleakridge' (Cobridge) and 'Bursley' (Burslem). The station itself is an architectural gem, a sort of Jacobean mansion with platforms where you would expect to find the croquet lawn. Across Winton Square, with its statue of Josiah Wedgwood, stands an equally imposing hotel. In the town itself the town hall and parish church make enduring architectural statements, but elsewhere the effect is largely lacklustre, and interest in the town is reliant on the proliferation of pottery works and factory shops.

Public Transport

TRAINS - major railhead adjacent to bridge 113. Tel: 01782 411411.

Boating Facilities

DOLPHIN BOATS - Old Whieldon Road, Stoke. Tel: 01782 49390. Gas, boat & engine sales, moorings, slipway, repairs & servicing.

EVERY city has its soft underbellys of suburbia, and HEM HEATH, notwithstanding the presence of a colliery on its doorstep, is one of Stoke's. Now in private ownership, the local mine was the scene of a poignant protest vigil by miner's wives opposed to British Coal's determination to close it in 1993. Happily, it now has a new lease of life under the auspices of Coal Investments. The low, un-numbered bridge north of bridge 108 used to carry a private railway into Michelin's tyre works on the far side of Trent Vale.

Another sort of industry altogether lies close to TRENTHAM LOCK, a deep chamber with an undertow when filling, which has alongside it the cellars of a demolished lock-keeper's house. The industry in question is the famous pottery works of Wedgwood. They moved to Barlaston from their original site at Etruria in 1940. The new plant departed from the traditional design of pottery works in many ways, not least the adoption of electric tunnel ovens in place of bottle kilns.

Blue brick abutments mark the course of the Trentham branch railway which, in its brief heyday, carried jam-packed excursions of North Staffordshire folk to the gardens of Trentham Hall. Trentham had been the seat of the Dukes of Sutherland, the most recent property having been completed in 1842 to the designs of Sir Charles Barry, architect of the Houses of Parliament. By all accounts it had been a most beautiful house set in the loveliest of landscaped parklands and Italian gardens. However, the Trent ran through these gorgeous grounds and, as the river grew more and more polluted by the combined effluents of The Potteries, life for the Duke, his household and visitors - which often included royalty - became

less and less idyllic. Eventually the Duke was forced to quit Trentham for another of the family seats, and the hall was demolished just before the Great War. He left the grounds to the people of the Potteries and, as more sophisticated methods of sewage control were developed, Trentham Gardens became a celebrated resort for the residents of North Staffordshire. A tall monument commemorating the second Duke of Sutherland can be seen rising above woodlands to the west of Trentham Lock.

The great Palladian facade of Barlaston Hall gazes benignly over the canal between bridges 103 and 104. Once there were fears that subsidence caused by mining at Hem Heath might bring about its demolition, but now it is in the process of being refurbished by English Heritage. Next door stands a church abandoned because of the same threat of subsidence. A new church, paid for by British Coal, has been erected in Barlaston village.

BARLASTON is a popular overnight mooring point, details of its facilities appear on page 23. At one time there was a busy boatbuilding yard here. A row of cottages occupied by its workforce remains on the off-side of the canal south of bridge 103.

BARLASTON

NEWS

103

"Plume of Feathers"

Barlaston Hall

Wedgwood Pottery & Visitor Centre

Barlaston

Key
1 Former boatbuilding yard

Site of Great Fenton collieries and ironworks

STOKE

8

incinerator

108

70'

Course of Michelin works rly

A500 to M6 Junct. 15

Hem Heath Colliery

A5035 from Longton

70'

Hem Heath

Course of Trentham Branch

106

105A

105

104A

"The Trentham"

A5035 to Trentham

70'

Trentham Lock No.35
11ft 11ins

104

70'

sewage works

103

STAFFORD

10

By-road to Tittensor & A34

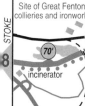

MAKING its way through the upper valley of the Trent, the canal encounters the market town of Stone, original headquarters of the Trent & Mersey Canal Company.

STONE lost its role as the administrative centre for the canal when it was bought out by the North Staffordshire Railway in 1846, but retained an extensive dockyard for maintenance purposes, whilst many of the town's once interesting array of industries used the canal for transport. Nowadays the emphasis is obviously on leisure use, and there is still much to see as you chug through the four locks of the Stone flight.

The top lock, known as LIMEKILN, is situated on the northern edge of town, near the railway station with its distinctive 'Dutch' gabled booking-hall and adjacent to Five Towns' boatbuilding yard enhanced by a delightful narrow-gauge railway. The next lock down is NEWCASTLE ROAD, overlooked by a large convent school; a boat horse tunnel leads underneath the road to a busy pound occupied by two hire fleets and linear moorings for private boats. The former ale stores of Joule's Brewery overlook the canal before it widens by a fascinating spread of docks, covered and uncovered, wet and dry. These belong to the Canal Cruising Company, a pioneer of boating holidays on the canals, having been founded in 1948. It was here that L.T.C. Rolt's famous boat, "Cressy", the true, inanimate hero of the book "Narrow Boat", met its end, being broken up and cremated after failing to pass a survey in 1951.

YARD LOCK, located beside the boatyard, is the deepest of the flight, and with one ground paddle takes a long time to fill. You can pass the minutes regarding the impressive architecture of the adjacent hospital, much of which predates the canal and was once the town's workhouse. The gas works stood beside the next pound on a site now given over to car parking. A restaurant boat operates from a neat brick wharf here.

STAR LOCK is the bottom chamber in the flight. The pub which gave it the name dates from the 16th century. An old warehouse on the offside below bridge 93 has been converted into retirement flats and several new buildings erected beside it in a pleasingly harmonious style. The canal company's offices stood alongside the towpath at this point, though there is little sign of this now. They were demolished after the war having been used for many years as a chocolate factory. Arguably the best moorings for access to the town are provided here, alongside a sportsground and children's play area.

There are also four locks in the MEAFORD FLIGHT; the locals say "Method". Originally three of them were combined as a 'staircase'. Traces of the old course of the canal can clearly be seen to the west of the present layout. Meaford Locks form an attractive group and are bordered by a country road with stone walling; one of the first signs that the Midlands are beginning to give way to the North. Meaford power station has been closed since our last edition and its cooling towers demolished.

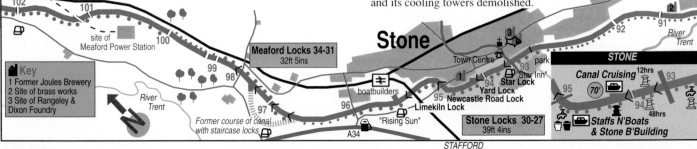

Stone

Key
1 Former Joules Brewery
2 Site of brass works
3 Site of Rangeley & Dixon Foundry

site of Meaford Power Station

Meaford Locks 34-31
32ft 5ins

Town Centre — park

Star Lock

"Star Inn"

Yard Lock

Newcastle Road Lock

Limekiln Lock

boatbuilders

"Rising Sun"

River Trent

Former course of canal with staircase locks

Stone Locks 30-27
39ft 4ins

STAFFORD

STOKE

STONE

Canal Cruising 12hrs

Staffs N'Boats & Stone B'Building

River Trent

A34

Stone

Stone is a bustling little market town with a rich and varied history. Conscious of their heritage, the local civic society have erected plaques on walls recalling that Peter de Wint, the landscape watercolourist, was born here; that the Duke of Cumberland came here to do battle; that the "Star Inn" has long attended to the thirst of passers-by; and that in roughly a hundred years from now a leading member of the community will be entitled to open a memory vault secreted in a cask beneath the old entrance arch of Joules Brewery. The demise of Joules remains Stone's great sadness. This proud independent had been brewing in the town since 1758 and, with the advent of the canal and the possibilities of export it brought, their ales became fashionable in Europe and the Americas. Once they operated a pair of boats to bring in coal for firing the steam plant. As late as the fifties their office retained the telephone number 'Stone 1'. But in 1970 they were taken over by the Bass Charrington conglomerate and, not unexpectedly, brewing ceased four years later, though the canalside ale stores remain intact. Bents, the town's other brewers, closed in the early 1960s.

Eating & Drinking

STAR INN - canalside bridge 93. Quaint lockside pub with a multitude of rooms all on seemingly different levels, especially after a pint or two of Banks's bitter. Inexpensive, but filling, bar meals. Breakfasts served daily ex Sun.
RISING SUN - adjacent Limekiln Lock. Families are welcome at this comfortable Bass pub. Bar lunches and dinners daily except Sundays. Canalside garden with swings etc.
CROWN HOTEL - High Street. Handsome 18th century coaching inn. Bar and restaurant meals.
AL SHEIKH'S - Lichfield Street. Balti restaurant in attractive modern brick & glass building. Table bookings on 01785 819684.
HATTERS - Newcastle Road (adjacent bridge 95). Wine bar open Tue-Sat evenings. Bookings on 01785 819292.

Shopping

Stone is a good shopping centre with the advantage of being so close to the canal that you can easily carry heavy carrier-bags back to the boat. Nice cakes from Hammersleys bakery on High Street.. Books from Old Fire Station bookshop at rear of Market Square.

Public Transport

BUSES - PMT every half hour to/from Stafford and Hanley. Tel: 01782 747000.
TRAINS - local trains to/from Stoke and Stafford. Tel: 01782 411411.

Boating Facilities

CANAL CRUISING COMPANY - Crown Street, Stone ST15 8QN. Tel: 01785 813982 & 812620. 2 to 8 berth hire craft (Blakes). Pumpout, diesel, gas and a full range of facilities including drydock.
STAFFORDSHIRE NARROWBOATS - Newcastle Road, Stone ST15 8JW. Tel: 01785 816871. 2 to 12 berth hire craft (Blakes). Pumpout, diesel etc.
STONE BOATBUILDING - as above. Tel: 01785 812688. Calor gas, diesel, slipway, comprehensive chandlery and gift shop.

Barlaston

(See Map 9) Suburbia has engulfed canalside Barlaston, but uphill over the level crossing, a by-road winds attractively through older parts of the village to Barlaston Hall and Wedgwood's pottery works, making for a pleasant short circular walk when combined with the towpath between bridges 103 and 104.

Eating & Drinking

PLUME OF FEATHERS - canalside bridge 103. An unprepossessing modern exterior disguises a welcoming Bass pub offering homemade 'farmhouse' dishes. There's a children's room and a garden with rabbits and a bowling green.

Shopping

Suburban row of shops west of bridge 103

Stone

including: chemist, Spar, butcher, greengrocer and newsagent.

Places to Visit

WEDGWOOD - adjacent bridge 104. Open Mon-Sat throughout the year plus Sundays in summer. Tel: 01782 204218. "Living museum, art gallery, gift shop, cinema, displays by skilled craftsmen."

Public Transport

TRAINS - deteriorating local service to/from Stoke and Stafford. Tel: 01782 411411. PMT bus service now provides much better link with Stoke.

TAKING apparent pleasure in each other's company, canal and river, road and railway make their undemonstrative way through a shallow valley, skirting, but scarcely encountering, a succession of small settlements, barely in the category of villages. With no great dramas to catch the eye, the canal traveller is thrown back on his own resources. He can pass the time wrestling with the great conundrums of life or anticipate the slow drawing of a pint in the cool bars of the "Greyhound" at Burston or the "Dog & Doublet" at Sandon. Frustratingly, it is more than likely that the 'he' in question will be a boater, rather than a walker, for the towpath leaves something to be desired. In fact, the banks are so eroded that in most places it is difficult to moor, or even to reach and pick the thick clumps of pink balsam flower that provide so much colour and musky scent as summer draws to a close.

ASTON LOCK marks the half-way point of the Trent & Mersey's route from Preston Brook to Shardlow; names which mean nothing now but were once as well known as Spaghetti Junction and Watford Gap. One of the distinctive cast-iron mileposts, originally made in Stone by Rangeley & Dixon, quotes 46 miles in either direction. Those that have been lost down the years have been replaced with replicas by the Trent & Mersey Canal Society; a laudable and imaginative contribution to conservation.

It's but a short walk from SANDON LOCK to the picturesque estate village of the same name. Sandon Hall, home of the Harrowbys, is a Victorian house in Jacobean style, well hidden from the world in rolling parkland. Above the woods peeps a slender urn-topped column commemorating William Pitt. Another Prime Minister, the assassinated Spencer Perceval, is remembered in a nearby shrine. Unfortunately the house and its grounds are rarely open to the public, but you can walk up the hill with the pheasants to the isolated church of All Saints to gain a panoramic view of the Trent Valley. Other points of interest in Sandon include the war memorial at the cross-roads, the quaint 'arts & crafts' style village hall and matching pub (which only recently condescended to dispense beer on the Sabbath) and the ornate former station house with its *porte-cochere* built to accommodate the carriage from Sandon Hall.

If you are travelling around a full circuit of the FOUR COUNTIES RING, it is rewarding to contrast the character of the Trent & Mersey with the Shropshire Union; barely ten miles across country to the west, but a world away in style and atmosphere. Here the canal winds apparently arbitrarily beneath mellow brick accommodation bridges in a Georgian apotheosis of grace, whilst the 'Shroppie', with its sturdy stone bridges, bold straights and Victorian sense of purpose, exudes an altogether different ambience.

Summary of Facilities

There are congenial country inns at Burston and Sandon: THE GREYHOUND (Burtonwood Ales) and DOG & DOUBLET (Ind Coope) respectively. Both do food, whilst the latter also offers accommodation. Sandon also has a useful roadside stores (stocking Wright's Pies!) and a post office. Mooring at Sandon is easy, either above or below the lock; Burston less so.

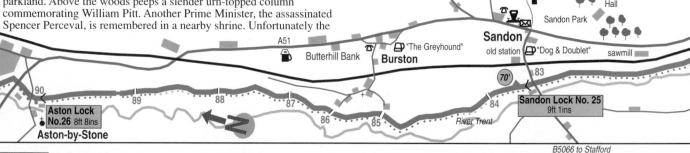

STOKE

A51

Butterhill Bank   "The Greyhound"   Sandon
                   Burston   old station   "Dog & Doublet"   sawmill
                                                              Hall
                                                    Sandon Park

10   90
      89   88   87   70'   83
           86   85   84   Sandon Lock No. 25
Aston Lock   9ft 1ins
No.26 8ft 8ins
Aston-by-Stone   River Trent

B5066 to Stafford

WANDERING through a gracious landscape, planned and planted for posterity by the gentry of Sandon, Weston and Ingestre, the Trent & Mersey Canal continues its relationship with the Trent Valley, basking in rural tranquility like a Sunday afternoon rambling club. Given the beauty of the countryside, it is no coincidence that several wealthy and influential families put down grandiose roots here. How did they perceive the arrival of Brindley's canal? Were they excited by its potential or fearful of its intrusion? History records that almost without exception the gentlemen of Staffordshire were in favour of the canal. Perhaps they saw only the financial advantages which might accrue from its construction, and not that it could be a precursor of change in their hitherto orderly and immutable world.

Any scar tissue wrought by the advent of the canal must have been well healed by the time the railways arrived. The North Staffordshire Railway followed the course of the Trent & Mersey (which it was soon to acquire) down the valley to Colwich and became a main line of some importance as a through route between Manchester and London via The Potteries. Another line arrived in the landscape, was

absorbed into the Great Northern Railway, and became a far flung outpost of the LNER at the grouping of the railway companies in 1923. Passenger traffic was never significant - how could it be in these rural haunts? - but the milk of the Trent Valley's cows was creamy enough for the scheduling of a daily milk train to the capital.

One activity in this otherwise rural area that the canal did help to prosper was the making of salt. The Trentside village of that name had associations with the trade going back to Medieval times; perhaps even Roman. But at both Shirleywich and Weston brine pumping developed significantly because coal could be brought in by canal to fuel evaporation and the finished product carried to its markets more expeditiously.

Weston-on-Trent

You can sit by the village green outside the CAMRA recommended WOOLPACK after a hard day's boating, whilst a mile along the A518 to the east lies AMERTON WORKING FARM, a centre for crafts and home cooking, easily reached by boaters with bicycles on board. The village's other pub, the SARACEN'S HEAD, also qualifies for inclusion in the "Good Beer Guide". Both pubs offer a wide range of food. The post office stores and newsagency is open daily (inc Sun am). WESTON ANTIQUE GALLERY (adjacent bridge 80) opens Wed to Sat and deals in antique maps, prints, pottery, porcelain, silver and glass etc. In place of those ghost trains, Stevenson's yellow buses run to Stafford and Uttoxeter. Tel: (01283) 544662.

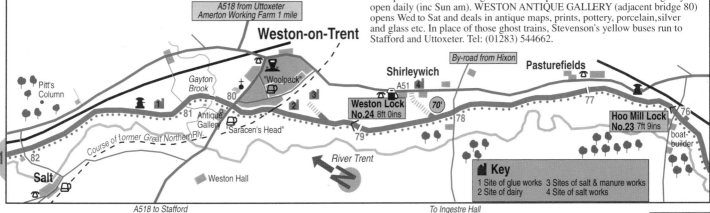

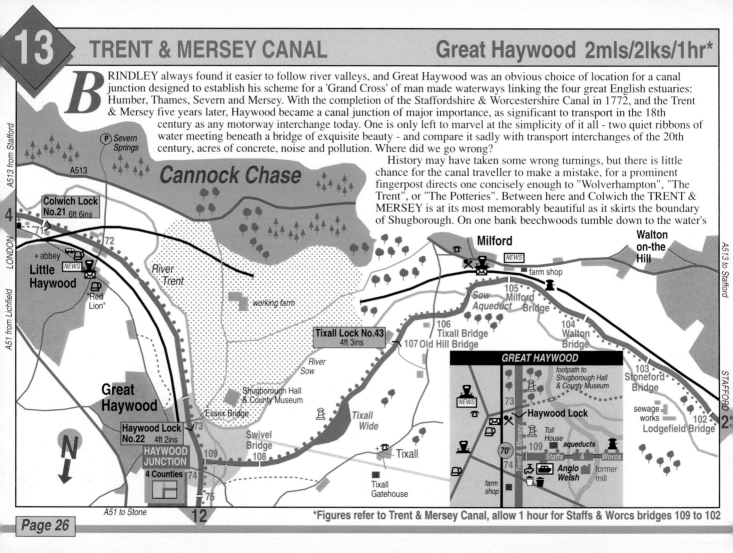

BRINDLEY always found it easier to follow river valleys, and Great Haywood was an obvious choice of location for a canal junction designed to establish his scheme for a 'Grand Cross' of man made waterways linking the four great English estuaries: Humber, Thames, Severn and Mersey. With the completion of the Staffordshire & Worcestershire Canal in 1772, and the Trent & Mersey five years later, Haywood became a canal junction of major importance, as significant to transport in the 18th century as any motorway interchange today. One is only left to marvel at the simplicity of it all - two quiet ribbons of water meeting beneath a bridge of exquisite beauty - and compare it sadly with transport interchanges of the 20th century, acres of concrete, noise and pollution. Where did we go wrong?

History may have taken some wrong turnings, but there is little chance for the canal traveller to make a mistake, for a prominent fingerpost directs one concisely enough to "Wolverhampton", "The Trent", or "The Potteries". Between here and Colwich the TRENT & MERSEY is at its most memorably beautiful as it skirts the boundary of Shugborough. On one bank beechwoods tumble down to the water's

Cannock Chase

Severn Springs

A513 from Stafford

A513

LONDON

4

71

Colwich Lock No.21 6ft 6ins

72

+ abbey

Little Haywood

NEWS

"Red Lion"

River Trent

working farm

Milford

Walton on-the Hill

NEWS

farm shop

A513 to Stafford

Sow Aqueduct

105 Milford Bridge

104 Walton Bridge

106 Tixall Bridge

107 Old Hill Bridge

Tixall Lock No.43 4ft 3ins

River Sow

Great Haywood

A51 from Lichfield

Shugborough Hall & County Museum

Essex Bridge

Swivel Bridge

108

Tixall Wide

Tixall

103 Stoneford Bridge

sewage works

102 Lodgefield Bridge

STAFFORD

2

Haywood Lock No.22 4ft 2ins

HAYWOOD JUNCTION

4 Counties

109

74

75

12

A51 to Stone

Tixall Gatehouse

GREAT HAYWOOD

footpath to Shugborough Hall & County Museum

NEWS

73

Haywood Lock

Toll House

70'

109

aqueducts

Staffs & Worcs

74

Anglo Welsh

former mill

farm shop

N

*Figures refer to Trent & Mersey Canal, allow 1 hour for Staffs & Worcs bridges 109 to 102

edge. On the other, across the Trent, there are glimpses of the curious statues, antiquities and follies which pepper the grounds of this famous home of the Anson family. COLWICH LOCK lies in an attractive setting between the village church, a picturesque farm and a bend in the river. From bridge 72 you can take an idyllic walk to Seven Springs and on up into The Chase itself.

Staffs & Worcs Canal

Through the arch of bridge 109 - an 18th century fusion of functional engineering and enduring loveliness - the Staffordshire & Worcestershire Canal can be seen heading westwards on its 46 mile journey down to the Severn at Stourport. Two aqueducts carry it across the Trent and a millstream. A couple of miles further on it crosses the Sow. Between these river crossings the canal suddenly casts of its inhibitions and widens into a broad lake of quite un-canal-like proportions, bordered by thick reedbeds inhabited by a gorgeous array of wildfowl. Boaters will find their craft looping the loop out of sheer exuberance. This is Tixall Wide or Broadwater and there are two theories for its surprising existence. Some maintain that the canal was widened into an artificial lake to placate the owner of Tixall Hall. Others that the expanse of water predates the canal, that it was naturally formed, and that Izaak Walton learnt to fish here. Whichever explanation suits you, don't miss the extraordinary Elizabethan gatehouse which overlooks the Wide. The hall itself, where Mary Queen of Scots was imprisoned for a fortnight in 1586, was demolished long ago.

Cont. on Map 23

The Haywoods

The villages of Great and Little Haywood are separated by the long, high brick wall of the Shugborough estate. dormitory housing has inevitably expanded both populations, but the centres remain peaceful and largely unspoilt; especially so in the charming lane leading from Great Haywood, under the railway and over the canal to the Essex Bridge, one of the finest examples of a packhorse bridge imaginable. On hot summer days the locals splash about in the water here as their forebears must have done for generations.

Eating & Drinking

LOCK HOUSE - adjacent Haywood Lock. Popular tea rooms and licenced restaurant.
A pair of pubs in either village.

Shopping

Little Haywood has a post office stores and newsagent. Great Haywood has two general stores, a post office, and a farm shop alongside the junction. At the junction the former toll house is an outlet for canalware and crafts.

Places to Visit

SHUGBOROUGH - access via Haywood Lock and Essex Bridge. Open daily April to December. Admission charge. Attractions include mansion, county museum, working farm, gardens, National Trust shop and cafeteria. a visit to the farm can be particularly recommended for families. Frequent special events and a regular point of departure for hot air balloons. Tel: 01889 881388.

Public Transport

BUSES - regular Midland Red service through LITTLE HAYWOOD to Stafford. Tel: 01785 223344.

Boating Facilities

ANGLO-WELSH - Leicester Road, Market Harborough LE16 7BJ. Tel: 01858 466910. (Boatyard 01889 881711) 2 to 10 hire craft and full range of boating facilities.

Milford

Useful facilities and access to Cannock Chase in a village bisected by the busy A513.

Great Haywood

THE river's slow influence pervades the canal, and the pair wander across the landscape like indolent lovers on a long afternoon, chaperoned at a discreet distance by the recumbent mass of The Chase. Several big houses were built by prosperous landowners in this enchanting countryside. The stuccoed facade of Bishton Hall overlooks the canal. Nowadays it is a prep school with a cricket ground shaded by ancient chestnut trees bordering the water. Another mansion, Wolseley Hall, stood opposite on the far bank of the river. It was demolished long ago, but the grounds have been restored as ornamental gardens. Wolseley Bridge has graced the Trent here since 1800. It was designed by John Rennie, best known in canal circles for his work on the Kennet & Avon. The "Staffordshire Way" joins the towpath at bridge 68 and follows the canal as far as Great Haywood, before disappearing off into the grounds of Shugborough on its way to the southernmost tip of the county at Kinver Edge.

RUGELEY gets a bad press from most guide-books which condescend to mention it at all, but we like the sheer up-front ugliness of the place, and it's refusal to pretend to be what it patently isn't; pretty! Once it had two dubious claims to fame: its malodorous tannery and its connections with the notorious Victorian poisoner, William Palmer. But the tannery and the poisoner no longer impinge, and it's the power station which dominates now, being opened here in the Sixties to take advantage of coal mined on the spot; though the colliery has closed and coal is brought in by train from goodness knows where these days. At Brindley Bank the canal suddenly stops running parallel with the Trent and turns sharply to cross it, as though Brindley had been screwing up his courage to bridge the river. A handsome pumping station overlooks this crossing of water over water, though the aqueduct itself is nothing to write home about.

By bridge 68 a short, reedy arm adjacent to the railway provides a useful turning point for lengthy craft. It occurs to us that this may have been used as a transhipment basin in the fledgling days of the railway, perhaps for the conveyance of building materials.

site of trans-shipment basin

B5013 from Abbot's Bromley

70'

68

69

River Trent

Trent Aqueduct

Bishton Hall School

Brindley Bank Pumping Station

LONDON

industrial estate

power station

67

2

Safeway Town Centre

66

3

industrial estate

4

Garden Park

70

Colwich

Ab1 from Stone CREWE

Stafford

3

Craft Centre

Wolseley

Key
1 Former mill
2 Site of tannery
3 Former mill
4 site of Lea Hall colliery

park

Rugeley

65

64

15

A1 to Lichfield

A460 to Cannock WALSALL

Rugeley

Rugeley

A thousand jobs were lost when Lea Hall Colliery closed in 1990, but this is a resilient little town well versed in the vicissitudes of existence. Life here is lived on the cheap, though with a certain deadpan dignity. A consoling beauty is to be found up on The Chase. Here in the tight-knit streets and on the old Coal Board estates is thrift and graft and a perverse civic pride.

Eating & Drinking

GEORGE & BERTIES - Albion Street. An unusual cafe with a central bar around which customers sit perched on high stools as if this were somewhere in Belgium.
LA TERRAZZA - Italian restaurant housed in old chapel on Lichfield Street.
ARIA - Anson Street. Take-away Balti.

Shopping

Moor north of bridge 66 for easiest access to nearby town centre. Large branch of Safeway nearby. Market on Tue, Thur-Sat. Most banks and lots of good cake shops.

Public Transport

BUSES - services throughout the Trent Valley and Cannock Chase. If you've time to spare take the Green Bus to Cannock, a magical mystery tour up and over The Chase. Tel: 01785 223344.
TRAINS - sparse weekday service along Trent Valley but much more frequent from newly re-opened Town station to Walsall and Birmingham. Tel: 01782 411411.

Colwich & Wolseley

Two little communities strung out along the A51. Wolseley has a craft centre, antiques showroom, art gallery and garden park all accessible from bridge 70. The nearby WOLSELEY ARMS does a wide range of food and is an attractive pub long ago used by the promoters of the canal for their meetings.

WHILST by no means a length of canal likely to endear itself to connoisseurs of the picturesque, this stretch of the TRENT & MERSEY is never actually overwhelmed by industry, and there are a number of invigorating views out over the Trent Valley or up on to the flanks of Cannock Chase. Armitage and Shanks are synonymous with toilet plumbing. Their trade marks are emblazoned on public conveniences throughout the world. Once they were separate firms, they merged in 1969, but the site alongside the canal at ARMITAGE dates back to 1817. Sanitaryware became a speciality in the 19th century under the management of Edward Johns - the origin of the Americanism "Going to the John." Today the factory is huge and convincingly prosperous, and Armitage Shanks are a public limited company with a seemingly 'watertight' future. Connections are apparent with another famous earthenware firm at Spode House and Hawkesyard Priory. Josiah Spode, a member of the North Staffordshire pottery family, left his house to a Dominican Order in 1893 and the monks proceeded to build a priory in the gounds. The priory is now a nursing home, but Spode House itself has been just another depressing property market statistic for some years, its gothic facade beginning to crumble in the face of continued disuse; though as we went to press there was talk that the house and grounds might become a golf course.

Passing beneath the A513, the canal narrows and negotiates a rocky cutting. One-way working is the order of the day. This was formerly the site of Armitage (or "Plum Pudding") Tunnel, a dramatic unlined bore through the rock face. Subsidence, brought about by coal mining, necessitated opening out of the tunnel, and concrete lining of the canal banks.

Handsacre

An unremarkable community, but the High Bridge spanning the Trent to the north of bridge 58 is worth a look; though unsightly girders are nowadays called upon to support its graceful single cast-iron arch made at Coalbrookdale in 1830. Facilities include THE CROWN, a congenial local where the local's repartee is apt to be as frothy as your pint of Bass. Children are catered for, but food is limited to snacks, though the chip shop, 100 yards up the road, is excellent.

Armitage

Guidebooks point to the "interesting" church perched on a rocky bluff above the bosky canal by bridge 61, but the village is dominated by the sanitaryware works. A path leads beneath the West Coast Main Line railway and over the Trent to the isolated settlement of Mavesyn Ridware. There are a number of shops on the main road, but mooring can be problematical on what is a rather narrow and tortuous secton of canal. A couple of canalside pubs vie for your custom: the PLUM PUDDING (bridge 61a) has dropped considerably below the level of the canal because of subsidence, but the outdoor patio remains commensurate with the canal: food is usually available and families are catered for. The ASH TREE INN by bridge 62 is a refurbished Banks's pub which has given its name to the local boating club. Should you need to throw money at a haemorrhaging morale, put on your best bib & tucker and repair to the OLD FARMHOUSE RESTAURANT across the road from the aforementioned "Plum Pudding"; table bookings on 01543 490353.

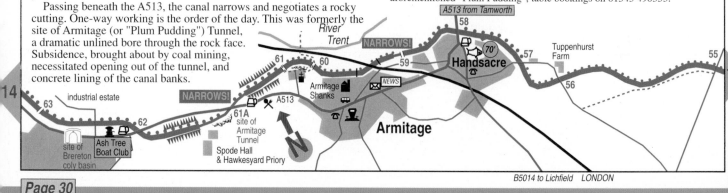

A BEND in the canal south of WOODEND LOCK, and glimpses of the three spires of Lichfield Cathedral, tell you that you and the Trent & Mersey have travelled as far south as you are ever going to get in the canal's arc-like journey between Preston Brook and Shardlow. Ravenshaw Woods are a riot of rhododendron colour in early summer. The works by bridge 54 was once the smelly "milk factory" referred to by L.T.C. Rolt in "Narrow Boat". Nowadays it's occupied by various light industries. There was also a wharf here for the village of Kings Bromley. The wharfingers house stands derelict, too far gone for rehabilitation as a residence, though a builder friend of ours did once consider it.

FRADLEY JUNCTION'S fame outweighs the sum of its parts. All that ever seems to change here are the records on the jukebox in "The Swan". On hot summer days the junction is hugely popular with sightseers attracted by the pub and the colourful comings and goings of canal craft through the locks, but on winter afternoons it isn't difficult to imagine how it must have looked in the latter days of cargo carrying.

The Coventry Canal heads of in a southerly direction towards Fazeley and Tamworth; a route covered in our "South Midlands" and "Stourport Ring" Canal Companions. British Waterways' local manager and his staff occupy the neat former 'company' maintenance yard located between Keeper's and Junction locks. On the opposite bank private woodland masks Fradley Reservoir built for the canal but rarely called upon to act as a feeder now.

Between Fradley and Alrewas the canal crosses former common-land and the flat nature of the adjoining fields engenders a feeling of emptiness. The canal curves endearingly through the picturesque village of ALREWAS, long ago a centre of basket weaving. At the tail of Alrewas Lock the canal merges with the River Trent for a short distance before the river disappears unnervingly over a large weir. The towpath is carried over the mill stream, the main channel of the river, and a succession of reedy backwaters by a series of metal footbridges which somehow create a Thames-like quality about the whole scene.

Fradley Junction

The epitome of a rural canal junction, Fradley is liable to attract more motorists that it can always comfortably deal with. The SWAN INN plays a key role in this popularity, catering manfully for customers whether they have come by water or road. A wide choice of food is almost always available and families are welcome.

Boating Facilities

SWAN LINE CRUISERS - Fradley Junction, Alrewas, Burton-on-Trent DE13 7DN. Tel: 01283 790332. Hire craft bookable direct or through Hoseasons. Full boatyard facilities, including drydock, and shop with chandlery, gifts and groceries.

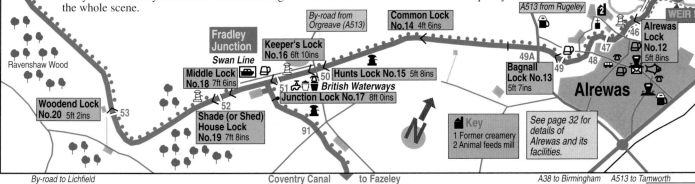

Alrewas

A pretty village which hasn't allowed itself to be entirely smothered by the grafting on of new housing. The animal feeds mill creates a welcome sense of local industry. Two famous waterway journalists, Harry Arnold and Robert Shopland, live in Alrewas, and it was from part of the mill that the short-lived, but much-missed, magazine "Narrow Boat" was published in the mid-Eighties.

Eating & Drinking

GEORGE & DRAGON - village centre. Quaint and convivial Marstons pub of considerable charm. Wide choice of bar meals Mon-Sat. Patio with childrens amusements.

RAFTERS RESTAURANT - as above. Plush restaurant adjunct to "George & Dragon". Reservations on 01283 790202.

THE NAVIGATION - adjacent Bagnall Lock. Bar and restaurant meals. Garden with swings and slides.

Two other pubs, a cafe and a fish & chip shop in the village.

Shopping

The village has some admirable shops. BARKERS (up along the main street towards the A38) has an unexpectedly ambitious selecton of wines and fine foods; COATES the butcher has a wide choice of game; whilst the bakery is excellent too. Other facilities include an off licence, chemist, newsagent and general store which stays open until 8pm Mon-Sat.

Public Transport

BUSES - Stevenson's to/from Burton and Lichfield Mon-Sat. Tel: 01785 223344.

Barton-under-Needwood

Mellifluously named but much enlarged village with good shopping facilities and several pubs approachable via footpath or B5016. THE BARTON TURNS (canalside by bridge 38) offers Pedigree and Guinness on draught but limited snacks.

Fradley Junction

KEEPING company with the Roman's Ryknield Street, the canal traverses the broad, flat valley of the Trent; a landscape of gravel pits and distant villages backed by low-lying hills.

Between Alrewas and WYCHNOR the canal suddenly assumes a quite different character as it negotiates a marshy, almost ethereal stretch of countryside, criss-crossed by drainage channels, or 'sitches', which thread their way through meadowlands to meet the Trent. It is a sudden, yet subtle, scene change. The domesticity of Alrewas village and the cacophony of the A38 are briefly forgotten, as the waterway puts you tantalisingly in touch with a past inhabited by eel-catchers, reed-cutters and sluice-keepers.

The Roman road has become the A38, a dual-carriageway carrying considerable traffic for which there are plans (aren't there always?) of upgrading to motorway standard. A likely victim of such a scheme would be the graceful Georgian building across the road from bridge 42, once a coaching inn known as "The Flitch of Bacon". Wychnor was the scene of a tradition, similar to the more famous one at Dunmow in Essex, whereby any man who could swear not to have wished to exchange his wife for

another woman, at any time during the first year of his marriage, was entitled to a flitch of bacon from the lord of the manor. It may - or may not - surprise you to learn that the flitch was never successfully claimed.

At BARTON TURNS wharves were provided for the villages of Barton and Walton, each a mile or so from the canal on opposite banks of the Trent. Good moorings are available here along with water and rubbish disposal facilities in a charming setting overlooked by a handsome Georgian wharf house. Quarter of an hour's walk away, Barton-under-Needwood itself is a useful spot for replenishing supplies. When the bridge across the river to Walton was damaged by floods in the 1940s, it was replaced by a 'temporary' Bailey bridge which is still in use.

TATENHILL LOCK lies in a deceptively remote setting. The former lock-keeper's house is now a private dwelling. A path runs from bridge 35 between old gravel workings, and through an fragrant pig farm, in the direction of the village of Tatenhill, tucked demurely away between folds of the Needwood Hills. There is no shop, but "The Horseshoe" is a particularly fine country pub, highly regarded for its food. The Forest of Needwood was once one of the largest royal hunting grounds. Little woodland now remains, though chunks of forest may return if the new National Forest ever comes to fruition.

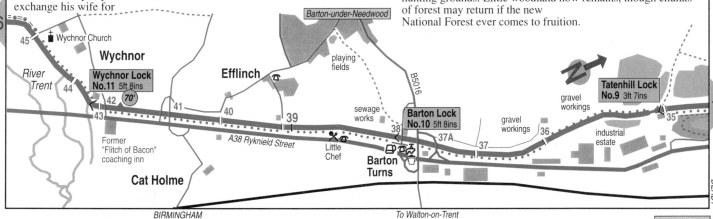

THE brewery town of Burton-on-Trent presides over the Trent & Mersey Canal's change of gauge: east of Dallow Lane the locks will be widebeam. When the canal opened in 1770, it brought a rapid decline in the use of the River Trent, which had itself been made navigable up to Burton at the beginning of the 18th century. To serve wharves established on the riverbank, however, a branch canal was built from Shobnall to Bond End. When the Birmingham & Derby Junction Railway was opened a drawbridge was provided to carry the line over this Bond End Canal. In 1846 a southbound train plunged into the canal because the bridge had been opened for the passage of a boat in the mistaken belief that no train was due!

Bridge 34 at BRANSTON is a popular mooring point for boaters attracted by the canalside pub. Beyond the towpath hedge the adjoining flooded-out gravel workings have been transformed into a 'water park' attracting a wide variety of wildfowl as well as a wide variety of the species anorak. Between Branston and SHOBNALL the canal runs at the foot of a ridge of hills marking the edge of what was once the Forest of Needwood. The semi-ruined house on the hill is known as Sinai Park. It belonged to the Benedictine monastery founded in the town in 1004. The main part of the abbey lay beside the river, but Sinai Park was used variously as a hunting lodge, summer house and blood-letting sanitorium.

It is at SHOBNALL that the canal traveller is made most aware of Burton-on-Trent's stock in trade. West of the canal stands Marston's brewery, to the east the Bass maltings. Visitors are quick to remark upon the aroma of hops in this vicinity, though locals are largely innured to the aromatic tang of the town. A common misapprehension is that Burton derives its excellence in brewing from Trent water. One look at the river is enough to confound that theory. In fact the water lies on beds of gypsum rock beneath the town and is pumped to the surface. This predominence of such stone made Burton a centre for the production of alabaster ornaments in the middle ages.

Playing fields border the outside of the canal between Shobnall and DALLOW LANE. One of the once numerous branch railways, linking the main lines with Burton's breweries and other industries, paralleled the canal on its way through the town. Nowadays it's used as a public footpath. In its heyday, Burton's 'internal' railway system was so dense that there were 32 level crossings in the town. The railways captured the bulk of beer transport from the canal, but at the end of the 18th century large volumes of ale were being exported via Hull to northern Europe, the Baltic and Russia, and via Liverpool to India and South America.

Until the late Seventies the basin at HORNINGLOW WHARF was overlooked by a salt warehouse, part of which actually spanned the canal, so that boats heading east seemed to disappear into a 'tunnel'.

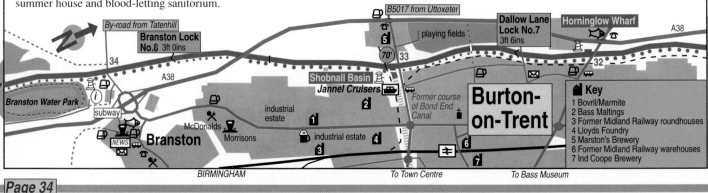

By-road from Tatenhill

Branston Lock No.8 3ft 0ins

B5017 from Uttoxeter

Dallow Lane Lock No.7 3ft 6ins

playing fields

Horninglow Wharf

A38

34

70'

33

A38

32

19

Branston Water Park

subway

Shobnall Basin

Jannel Cruisers

Former course of Bond End Canal

Burton-on-Trent

industrial estate

McDonalds

Morrisons

Branston

NEWS

industrial estate

BIRMINGHAM

To Town Centre

To Bass Museum

Key
1 Bovril/Marmite
2 Bass Maltings
3 Former Midland Railway roundhouses
4 Lloyds Foundry
5 Marston's Brewery
6 Former Midland Railway warehouses
7 Ind Coope Brewery

Burton-on-Trent

It is difficult to write dispassionately about one's home town. Affection collides with contempt; and there are casualties. But with a courteous nod in the direction of Tadcaster, Hook Norton and Southwold, this is the definitive brewery town. At the turn of the century there were over twenty companies with breweries in the town; the famous and the forgotten: Allsopp, Bass, Boddington, Charrington, Everard, Ind Coope, Marston, Salt, Truman, Worthington. But mergers and rationalisation have today reduced this to just three large concerns - Bass Ind Coope and Marstons - plus a small independent. So "Beertown-on-Trent" still reverberates to its stock in trade, though for anyone who knew it prior to the contraction of the brewing industry and the closure of its quaint network of interconnecting railway lines, the place is an 'Indian Pale' shadow of its former self. One of the most regretable casualties of progress has been the bulk of Burton's brewing infrastructure. Compare the fascinating model in the Bass Museum with reality, and you too will mourn the loss of so many maltings and brewing plants. Nowadays the most pleasant aspects of the town are to be had from the riverside. Perhaps it was always so, for this was where the monks chose to erect their vanished abbey.

Eating & Drinking

THE ALBION - third of a mile to north of Shobnall Basin. Large refurbished Marstons pub, good for families. Wide range of food, nice large garden.
BURTON BRIDGE BREWERY - mile south of Horninglow Wharf. Worth the long trek to sample the town's micro-brewery proudly flaunting its independence in the faces of the big boys. Unspoilt atmosphere, lunchtime snacks.
COOPER'S TAVERN - Cross Street (2nd right beyond railway station). Classic ale house with tap room.
THE BREWHOUSE - Union Street. Arts Centre cafe/restaurant serving lunches ex Mon.
PINOCCHIOS - Bargate. Italian restaurant. Tel: 01283 537526.

Shopping

The town centre is 15-20 dispiriting minutes walk from the canal, though buses operate from both Horninglow and Shobnall basins. Showpiece of the shopping area is the OCTAGON CENTRE, fairly typical of recent precinct designs, but notable for the charming clock which pays homage to the local brewing industry and the town's patron saint, St Modwen. Closer at hand there are shops along the length of Waterloo Street - easily reached from Dallow Lane and Shobnall and branches of Lloyds and Midland banks adjacent to the railway station. Market days on Thur, Fri & Sat.

Places to Visit

TOURIST INFORMATION CENTRE - New Street. Tel: 01283 516609.
BASS MUSEUM - Horninglow Street (10 mins walk from Horninglow Wharf) Tel: 01283 542031. Open daily, admission charge. Fascinating displays of the development of Burton brewing with the emphasis, not surprisingly, on Bass and Worthington. Shire horse and rail and road transport exhibits. Charming model of the town at the turn of the century with self-operating miniature trains. Mock-up of Horninglow Wharf in its heyday. Excellent catering facilities; ideal for lunch.
HERITAGE BREWERY - Anglesey Road (7 minutes walk from Shobnall Basin). Tel: 01283 569226. Delightful working brewery in premises dating from 1881.

Public Transport

BUSES - local services throughout the Trent Valley. Tel: 01543 577099.
TRAINS - hourly local service to/from Birmingham, Derby & Nottingham. Tel: 01332 257000.

Boating Facilities

JANNEL CRUISERS - Shobnall Marina, Burton-on-Trent, Staffs DE14 2AU. Tel: 01283 542718. 2 to 8 berth hire craft (Hoseasons). Full boatyard facilities including moorings and drydock.

Branston

Once a village, and ostensibly (though probably not) the birthplace of the eponymous pickle relish, now merely a suburb useful for its facilities.

Eating & Drinking

BRIDGE INN - canalside bridge 34. Charmingly small former boatman's pub where draught "Pedigree" is still served straight from the barrel. Good choice of inexpensive bar meals and a convivial atmosphere.
Through the underpass, Branston also boasts a fish & chip shop, a Chinese take-away and two other pubs.

Shopping

Use the subway beneath the road interchange to reach the shops, 5 minutes walk from bridge 34. Facilities include: 'early-late' store, post office, butcher and newsagent.

Places to Visit

BRANSTON WATER PARK - canalside. 40 acre lake transformed from former gravel pit. Visitor centre, nature trail, children's play area and picnic tables.

Repton & Willington

(Map 19) A useful watering hole with a trio of cosy pubs, Co-op store, post office and newly re-opened railway station, Willington's real significance lies in its proximity to the ancient settlement of Repton on the far bank of the Trent. Pinpointed by the slender spire of St Wystans, Repton is a worthwhile quarter of an hour's walk from the canal. The church is of Saxon origin, Repton having been the capital of Mercia in the 9th century until laid waste by marauding Danes. Nowadays the village is best known for its public school, location for the 1939 version of "Goodbye Mr Chips". Several good inns and a pleasant farmhouse tearoom can provide sustenance prior to the walk back.

EAST of Burton, the Trent & Mersey doesn't exactly flaunt its freshly acquired wide-beam status. True, the bridge-holes are more buxom, but it is not until Stenson Lock is reached, that the true gauge of the canal manifests itself. Barge wide vessels traded upwards from Nottingham to Horninglow until the railways took grip of the trade in beer; thereafter, even narrowboat traffic dwindled between Fradley and Shardlow: one of the last regular consignments was of cardboard for the manufacture of cigarette papers by Players at Nottingham.

Bridge 31 carries a link road occupying the trackbed of the North Staffordshire Railway's Burton to Tutbury branchline, haunt of a push & pull shuttle known as "The Jinnie". Beyond Stretton the course of the line has become a footpath and nature reserve. Rubber making is a lesser-known facet of the brewery town's economy, though the canalside Pirelli plant has shed much of its workforce in recent times.

Crossing the boundary between Staffordshire and Derbyshire, marked by an old mill race, the canal crosses the Dove upon a low-slung aqueduct of little aesthetic significance other than the usual invigoration of water spanning water. Beloved of Izaak Walton, the River Dove is virtually at journey's end here, being less than a mile from its lonely confluence with the Trent amidst low-lying pasturelands; all a far cry from the glories of Dovedale and the Peak District. An adjacent roadbridge, reputedly built by the monks of Burton Abbey, compensates for the aqueduct's plain looks. On sultry summer days local youths swim in this reach of the Dove, in spite of dangerous whirlpools in the vicinity. Pillboxes are another feature of the lower reaches of the Dove. Waterways, man-made and natural, were considered strategic lines of defence during the Second World War.

An imposing Georgian wharf house overlooks bridge 26 and the site of Egginton's old village wharf. Otherwise the canal is largely featureless as it makes its way through the Trent Valley, as if handcuffed by the portly escorts of a busy dual-carriageway and a main line railway. A pleasant ridge dominates the southern horizon, leading to the stiletto-fine spire of Repton church.

WILLINGTON, a commuter village dominated by its power station, seems to have set out its stall to attract canal visitors, the site of an old rail/canal transhipment wharf having been landscaped and provided with parking spaces for both boats and cars.

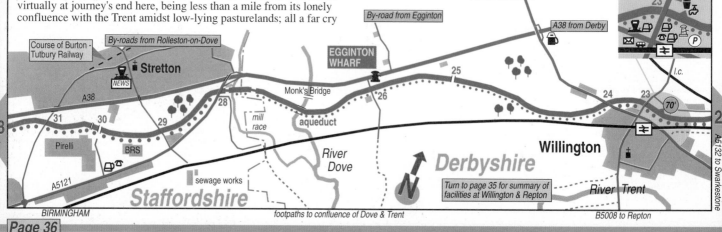

Turn to page 35 for summary of facilities at Willington & Repton

ARGUABLY at its most prosaic, the Trent & Mersey makes its way between Willington and Swarkestone with the world-weary demeanour of a man who has walked the same dog around the same municipal park twice a day for a dozen years. Intermittent trains break the monotony, but if your adrenalin doesn't flow at the thought of a 'fifty-six' thrumming by with a payload of slack from what's left of the Nottinghamshire coalfield, then it's time to go below and make the bacon sandwiches.

Coal comes in by train to Willington Power Station too, though perhaps not for much longer, as this is another of the smaller generating plants likely to give way gracefully to the 'rush for gas'. Thankfully masked by the brow of an opportune hill, a huge Toyota car plant occupies much of the site of Derby's long lost municipal airport alongside the A38 beyond the village of Findern.

STENSON is well known in boat circles for its large mooring basin, deep wide-beam lock, and a trip-boat called "The Bubble".

Between Stenson and Swarkestone the canal, arm in arm with a railway line used chiefly by goods trains avoiding the centre of Derby, slinks furtively through fields given over to vegetable growing. Trudging the towpath one wet and windy January day, we paused to watch oil-skin-clad figures picking winter leeks.

The feeling that one is a long way from anywhere is misleading. Derby lies just over the rim of the northern horizon. But then canals have a knack of conjuring a stimulating sense of isolation in the most unpromising of circumstances.

From bridge 18, footpaths lead over arable fields to the forgotten Trentside village of Twyford. Once there was a ferry here. The posts which held the chain still stand. An old photograph of this one adorns our stairs. The ferry, flat-decked, fine-bowed and fairly wide of beam is being worked across with the aid of a fixed chain and the river's residual current. A man and boy are occupied with the machinations of the chain whilst two long-skirted ladies - one in a straw boater - hold the reins of a horse and trap. They might, perhaps, have been on their way to Repton for groceries. Frozen for posterity, they represent a pace of life obliterated by the development of road transport. And so, on your archaic canal boat, do you!

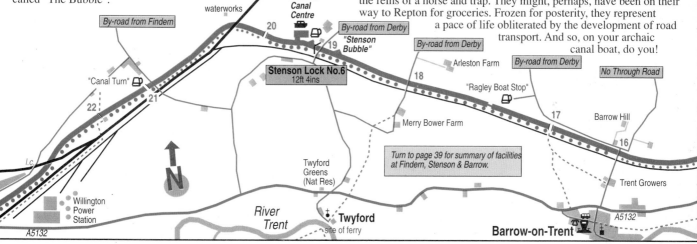

By-road from Findern

waterworks

Midland Canal Centre

By-road from Derby

"Stenson Bubble"

20

19

By-road from Derby

Arleston Farm

By-road from Derby

"Canal Turn"

Stenson Lock No.6
12ft 4ins

18

No Through Road

22

21

"Ragley Boat Stop"

17

Barrow Hill

16

Merry Bower Farm

CREWE

l.c.

Twyford Greens
(Nat Res)

Turn to page 39 for summary of facilities at Findern, Stenson & Barrow.

Trent Growers

9

Willington Power Station

River Trent

Twyford
site of ferry

Barrow-on-Trent

A5132

A5132

2

NEVER more than half a mile away from the Trent, and often closer, the canal travels through mellow countryside, much of which is given over to market-gardening.

Evidence of occupation by the Beaker People sixteen hundred years before the birth of Christ suggests that man's influence on Swarkestone goes a long way back. Swarkestone Bridge is of relatively modern origin, dating only back to the 12th century. It is generally regarded as the longest stone-built bridge in Britain. In 1347 the scale of tolls quoted charges of a ha'penny for a cask of sturgeons. In 1745 this was the furthest south that Bonnie Prince Charlie's army got in their attempt to capture the throne of England.

Just twenty-five years later the Trent & Mersey was being dug, and soon afterwards Swarkestone became the site of a junction with the Derby Canal, including a branch down to the river which only survived until around 1800.

The Derby Canal, overlooked by nationalisation in 1947, was acrimoniously abandoned in 1964, though trade had ceased twenty years earlier. The company who owned the canal were well aware that more money could be made from property deals than from running a public waterway. The old junction house remains intact, used, like the one at Huddlesford on the Coventry Canal, by a local boat club. The Derby Canal's towpath has been resurfaced as part of the Derby Cycle Route and a group has ambitions of restoring at least part of the canal to navigable standards.

By Weston Cliffs the canal glides through tumbling woodland. While construction of the canal was proceeding eastwards, a wharf was erected here for the transfer of goods from barge to riverboat. Later it was used for the transhipment of gypsum bound from Aston to King's Mills, whereupon, after being ground, the resultant plaster was despatched back up to the canal for consignment via Swarkestone and the Derby Canal to a builder's merchant in Derby.

In these days of the ubiquitous lorry, the amazing complexity and labour-intensiveness of previous eras of transport boggles the mind.

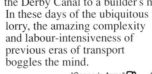

Map labels:

Course of Derby Canal & Derby Cycle Route

A514 from Derby

SWARKESTONE STOP

S.B.C.

Swarkestone Lock No.5
10ft 11ins

Course of Derby & Ashby Railway

70'

15 14 13

Cuttle Bridge

N

Course of former link with Trent

Swarkestone

River Trent

Hall

12

Derby Cycle Route

ruin

Swarkestone Bridge

Sailing Club

Stanton by Bridge

A514 to Swadlincote

Course of Derby & Ashby Railway

viaduct

viaduct

70'

11

site of Military Railway depot

Ukrainian Centre

Weston Cliffs

social club

10

site of Bridging School

former wharf

Derby Cycle Route
(Melbourne 1 mile)

By-road from Aston-on-Trent

Weston Grange

7

"Cooper's Arms"

Weston-on-Trent

"Old Plough"

8

9

Weston Lock No.4
10ft 11ins

site of lock

Derbyshire

River Trent

site of ferry

King's Mills

Leics.

22

By-road to Castle Donington

During the Second World War this dreamy riparian landscape was rudely awakened by the construction of an army camp at Weston Cliffs. It was built to house the army's railway engineers who operated the Melbourne and Ashby line as a military railway during the Second World War. The army camp also provided accommodation for soldiers attached to a Bridging School opened across the river at King's Newton. As part of their training they built a now vanished suspension bridge across the river to facilitate access between the camp and the school. The enigmatic remains of a steam crane used by the bridge-makers remains by the handsome cast-iron railway viaduct which now carries the Derby Cycle Route across the Trent near bridge 11. The trackbed of that line has been imaginatively resurfaced by Sustrans (the Bristol-based railway path and cycle route construction company) to create a traffic-free link between Derby and the handsome old market town of Melbourne.

Hardly had the railway engineers marched away, before the camp was commandeered to house Ukrainian refugees. Several hundred arrived here to escape oppression in their homeland in 1944. Some of them have never left. Weston Rectory, visible on its low hilltop to the north of the canal, is used as a home for the centre's more elderly residents, whilst parts of the camp are now used by Ukrainian youth groups. A number of Russian children were accommodated here following the Chernobyl nuclear disaster. Incidentally, the centre's social club - at which visitors, we're told, are made very welcome - was formerly an old boatman's pub.

The lane from bridge 8, by Weston Lock, provides easy access to the facilities of Weston village in one direction. In the other it offers a peaceful walk down to the site of an old lock opposite King's Mills, a popular bathing spot until demolition of a weir in 1957 rendered such activities dangerous. Rummage in the undergrowth and you may discern the remains of the old lock. There was a ferry here too, providing access to the mills on the Leicestershire bank of the Trent. Now the smart restaurant housed in the refurbished mill buildings might as well be on the moon as far as Derbyshire folk are concerned.

Findern

Formerly "The Greyhound", the CANAL TURN is an Ansells house popular with boaters and motorists alike. Food, children's play room , garden, and "non-stop video music in the cellar."

Stenson

Well known canal centre with pub, trip-boat and extensive moorings. THE BUBBLE , a pub converted out an old barn, does lunches.

Boating Facilities

MIDLAND CANAL CENTRE - Stenson, Derby Tel: 01283 701933. Full range of boat servicing facilities with emphasis on boatbuilding and sales. Moorings and gift shop

Barrow

RAGLEY BOAT STOP is a relatively new pub converted from an old farmhouse. Customer moorings are provided on the offside and the pub provides a wide range of inexpensive food lunchtimes and evenings daily. Pedigree and Directors on draught. Children's play facilities.

Swarkestone

Trent-side village with comfortable country inn called the CREW & HARPUR but no shopping facilities other than a garage on the A514. Ruined pavilion associated with now demolished hall visible in fields to south of canal.

Weston

The second Weston-on-Trent that the Trent & Mersey meets on its travels - the other one's on Map 12 near Stone.

Eating & Drinking

COOPERS ARMS - Weston Hall. Recently opened pub housed in 17th century mansion used by Cromwell as a temporary barracks. During the First World War an escaped German prisoner hid here briefly before eventually making his way back to his homeland. Bass beers and a wide choice of food.
OLD PLOUGH - traditional village centre pub. Ansells & food.

Shopping

Post office store open Mon-Sat (EC Wed).

Shardlow

(Map 22) Attractive Georgian village marred only by the busyness of the A6. Shardlow Hall was built in 1684 by Leonard Fosbrook from profits made on the river trade.

Eating & Drinking

HOSKINS WHARF - adjacent lock. Handsome warehouse refurbishment by Leicester brewer of the same name. Several bars, wide range of food.
MALT SHOVEL - Camra recommended tradtional pub offering good lunches and Marston's.
Two more pubs and two restaurants add further variety to Shardlow's catering facilities.

Boating Facilities

DOBSONS - The Wharf, Shardlow DE7 2GJ. Tel: 01332 792271. Wide range of boatyard facilities and well-stocked chandlery.
SHARDLOW MARINA - London Road, Shardlow . Tel: 01332 792832. Sales and moorings.
SAWLEY MARINA - Long Eaton, Notts NG10 3AE. Tel: 0115 973 4278. Extensive boating facilities and sales.

Shardlow

NAVIGATION from the Trent to the Mersey must have seemed like a proclamation for travel from the earth to the moon, but this was how the fledgling canal company advertised its purpose back in 1780. The words still adorn the largest warehouse at SHARDLOW, the company's 'inland port', once known waggishly as "Rural Rotterdam". And Shardlow, unlike its counterpart at the other end of the Trent & Mersey, has been fortunate enough to retain the greater part of its historic infrastructure. Pride of place goes to the handsome Clock Warehouse alongside Shardlow Lock. Dating from 1780 it now houses a pub, though having been restored in 1980 as a canal museum. But like many of Shardlow's warehouses, it really owes its survival to F.E. Stevens, a local animal feeds merchant, whose occupation of this, and several other canalside buildings, secured a use for them in the century which passed between the cessation of canal trade around 1879 and a new era of refurbishment for leisure and commercial use.

Although it is Shardlow which appears on the distinctive Trent & Mersey mileposts, the actual junction with the Trent Navigation is at Derwent Mouth, approximately a mile and a half east of the village, and it would be remiss of us not to guide you gently over the

Trent & Mersey's equivalent of a musical coda. It's a short journey, as easily accomplished on foot as afloat, for a footpath follows a navigable reach of the Trent back upstream from Derwent Mouth to Cavendish Bridge, creating a three mile walk of intriguing contrast between man-made and natural waterway. An imposing concrete horse-bridge, emblazoned with the initials of the Trent Navigation and dated 1932, carries the towpath across the Trent opposite its confluence with the Derwent. The latter looks alluring, but has not been practically navigable since the late eighteenth century. Downstream the Trent sweeps haughtily towards Nottingham, an eye-opener for boaters passing through Derwent Mouth Lock and away from the cosy world of the canals. A mile to the east lies Sawley Bridge Marina with its extensive facilities.

But all this belongs to another, as yet unpublished, Canal Companion and you must wend your way back with us along that Trentside footpath to where the old Cavendish Bridge brewery looks forlornly over the uppermost navigable reach of the river. Before the first bridge spanned the river here from 1759 onwards, Wilden Ferry carried the turnpike's traffic over the Trent at this point. The original bridge was washed away by floods in 1947. Now the A6's hurrying motorists roar across a concrete bridge with little pretensions of beauty, and then the majority of them roar through Shardlow too. One of those cars could get you back to Preston Brook in less than three hours, whereas a boat would take five working days. But then that's not the point is it?

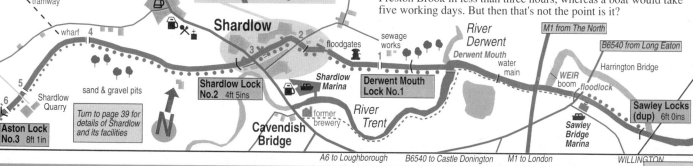

Turn to page 39 for details of Shardlow and its facilities

STAFFS & WORCS

Evening moorings on Tixall Wide

THE canal slips largely unmolested through the outskirts of Stafford. The county town stood an aloof mile to the west of the Staffs & Worcs Canal which, in true Brindley fashion, followed the easy contours of the Penk valley. Plans to construct a branch were dropped in favour of a simple lock down into the Sow, the river being dredged and realigned to take boats as far as a terminal basin at Green Bridge in the centre of Stafford. The navigation was opened in 1816 and in use until the end of the First World War. A footpath follows the riverbank into the town centre, but it's difficult to imagine how seventy foot narrowboats ever got up there!

Stafford Boat Club, with their substantial and impressive club house, occupy a former brickworks arm near Hazelstrine Bridge. The inherent other-worldliness of the canal undergoes strange fluctuations in fortune. Nowhere could be more apparently remote than Deptmore Lock, where the reclusive inhabitant of the rose-clad cottage commutes to the outside world by dinghy. Elsewhere, though, the M6 threatens to intrude like an unwelcome caller on your afternoon off; whilst Acton Trussell, which you'd expect with such a name to be a picture book English village, disappoints with its banal modern architecture. Similarly Wildwood, which ought to be the home of friendly, furry little creatures straight out of some children's tale, has become a housing estate on a hill. But when vapours rise of the Penk, and its marshy meadows ooze sponge-like with excess water, a return to an older, more elemental existence seems somehow tangible, and man's scars upon the landscape recede into the mists of time.

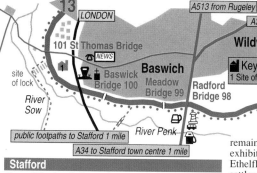

Stafford

One of England's lesser-known county towns, Stafford has always been too self-effacing for its own good; though there are signs now that it is waking up to its tourist potential. The centre is over a mile from the canal at Radford Bridge, but there are frequent buses, and those with time at their disposal will find a visit to Stafford rewarding. First stop should be the Ancient High House in Greengate Street - the main thoroughfare - which houses the Tourist Informaton Centre. Dating from 1595, it's thought to be the largest timber-framed town house remaining in England. Inside there is a heritage exhibition tracing Stafford's history since 913 when Ethelfleda, daughter of Alfred the Great, fortified the settlement against marauding Danish invaders. King Charles I stayed at the High House in 1642, and in later years Izaak Walton visited relatives who owned it. A town trail leaflet is available to guide you around the best of Stafford's surprisingly rich roll-call of historic buildings.

Eating & Drinking

THE SOUP KITCHEN - Church Lane. Quaint and bustling eatery serving coffees, lunches and teas.
PASTICHE - Mill Street. Coffee house and bistro (Thur, Fri & Sat evenings).

STAFFORD ARMS - Railway Street.. Real ale buff's pub serving Stoke brewed "Titanic" range and guest beers. Food too.
THE MOAT HOUSE - bridge 92 at Acton Trussell. Appealing restaurant & bar in former moated farmhouse. Guest beers. Lovely garden. Customer moorings.

Shopping

Good shopping centre featuring all the well known 'high street' names plus many attractive individual shops tucked away down twisting side streets.

Information

TOURIST INFORMATION - Ancient High House, Greengate Tel: 01785 40204
BUSES - Midland Red & PMT Tel: 01543 577099
TRAINS - Important railhead. Tel: 01782 411411

LOCKS come thick and fast as the canal ascends to, or descends from, its summit level. The motorway retreats, only to be replaced by the housing estates which cling-wrap the otherwise agreeable little town of Penkridge. Yet, a mile on either side, the countryside is characterised by rolling farmland lifting to the bulwark of Cannock Chase. The towpath between bridges 90 and 86 is hijacked by the "Staffordshire Way", part of its 92 mile journey from Mow Cop to Kinver Edge; both being extremities with canal connotations. Its path has come down off The Chase and across Teddesley Park. Teddesley Hall was demolished in the fifties following its wartime use as a prison camp for German officers. Bridge 89 once had ornate balustrades commensurate with its importance as the gateway to the hall, but sadly these have been infilled by brickwork.

Two hire bases increase boating activity on this length and boats tend to congregate at Penkridge Wharf for the taking on of water. Littleton colliery has closed, so no longer are long trains of coal wagons shunted across the canal south of Otherton Lock. Once the canal shared in this traffic too, and there was an extensive basin where coal was loaded from a central pier by gravity on to day boats bound for the Black Country. In the days before nationalisation of the coal industry, Littleton mine had such a poor safety record that it was nicknamed 'Slaughter Pit'.

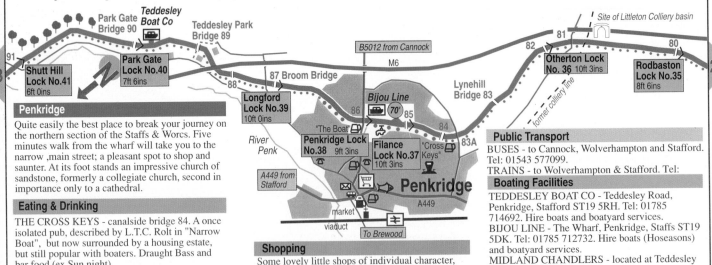

Penkridge

Quite easily the best place to break your journey on the northern section of the Staffs & Worcs. Five minutes walk from the wharf will take you to the narrow ,main street; a pleasant spot to shop and saunter. At its foot stands an impressive church of sandstone, formerly a collegiate church, second in importance only to a cathedral.

Eating & Drinking

THE CROSS KEYS - canalside bridge 84. A once isolated pub, described by L.T.C. Rolt in "Narrow Boat", but now surrounded by a housing estate, but still popular with boaters. Draught Bass and bar food (ex Sun night).
THE BOAT - canalside bridge 86. Attractively refurbished pub overlooking the wharf and Penkridge Lock. Home-cooking.

Shopping

Some lovely little shops of individual character, plus a small supermarket too. Lloyds and Barclays banks on A449. Thriving outdoor market on Wednesdays & Sundays beside the river.

Public Transport

BUSES - to Cannock, Wolverhampton and Stafford. Tel: 01543 577099.
TRAINS - to Wolverhampton & Stafford. Tel:

Boating Facilities

TEDDESLEY BOAT CO - Teddesley Road, Penkridge, Stafford ST19 5RH. Tel: 01785 714692. Hire boats and boatyard services.
BIJOU LINE - The Wharf, Penkridge, Staffs ST19 5DK. Tel: 01785 712732. Hire boats (Hoseasons) and boatyard services.
MIDLAND CHANDLERS - located at Teddesley Boat Co. Tel: 01785 712437. Stockists of extensive range of chandlery and boating equipment. Mail order service too.

Otherton

CALF HEATH is a strangely isolated tract of country, pancake flat and crossed by a grid of sullen little roads, with here and there a huddle of houses, gathered reassuringly together like something out of Van Gogh's early potato field paintings. The canal all but boxes the compass of this gravel pit-riddled landscape, so that the Chase with its communications tower and the chemical works with its phalanx of flaring chimneys, appear to move about you, teasing you into geographic insecurity, like a game of Blind Man's Buff.

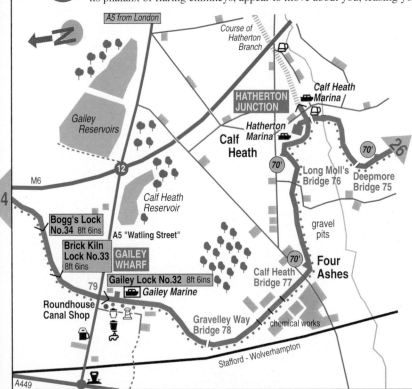

The last load of Cannock coal came off the Hatherton Branch in 1949 and it was abandoned a couple of years later. However, the illusion of a junction remains, because the bottom lock (of what was once a flight of eight in three miles) is still used to provide access to moorings. A preservation group is actively seeking restoration of the branch with the intention of linking it with the northern waters of the BCN at Norton Canes.

Watling Street crosses the canal at Gailey. The most significant feature here is the 'round house' which is now a splendid canal shop. There is something spellbinding about cylindrical buildings - Martello towers, windmills, lighthouses; even Birmingham's Bull Ring Rotunda - and Gailey round house, in its lock-side setting, has a particular charm which you will want to try and capture on film.

Summary of Facilities

GAILEY ROUND HOUSE stocks an excellent range of gifts, books and maps, together with a modest, but useful, selection of groceries and Sunday (but not daily) newspapers.

Boating Facilities

GAILEY MARINE - The Wharf, Watling Street, Gailey, Stafford ST19 5PR. Tel: 01902 790612. Hire craft (member of Blue Riband Club), pumpout and a range of other boatyard services.
CALF HEATH MARINA - Kings Road, Calf Heath WV10 7DU. Tel: 01902 790570. Pumpout, diesel, gas, bar & restaurant.
HATHERTON MARINA - Kings Road, Claf Heath. Tel: 01902 791887 or 0831 153 028. Moorings, drydock, boatbuilding, repairs & servicing.

*T*HE canal exchanges the loneliness of Calf and Coven heaths for the industrial and suburban outskirts of Wolverhampton; the M54 to Telford forming an obvious, though not intentional, boundary.

At Cross Green a former canal pub called "The Anchor" has become a popular steak bar and many boaters choose to moor here overnight. As it passes beneath the M54 the canal crosses the county boundary between Staffordshire and the West Midlands, one of the new counties which had its origins in the local government changes of 1974. Many people still mourn the old counties. It must have been galling, for instance, to have lived in Lincolnshire all one's life and wake up one morning in South Humberside. West Midlands was possibly the dullest of all the new names, and sounds as though it must have been the compromise of a committee. Black Country would have been a far more appropriate and resonant title. You can imagine its inhabitants enjoying

a perverse pride in such a name, no-one could possibly show a flicker of interest in anyone who admitted to coming from the West Midlands!

The most significant feature of this length is "Pendeford Rockin", the old boatmen's name for a shallow, but tellingly narrow cutting hewn by Brindley's navvies through a solid belt of sandstone which breaks through the clay strata at this point. The cutting, half a mile or so long, restricts the channel to such a degree that you begin to wonder if you have lost concentration and taken a wrong turn. There are, however, one or two passing places - as on a single lane road - where oncoming boats can be succesfully negotiated without losing one's temper. Similar narrows occur on the Shropshire Union north of Autherley as that canal encounters the same difficult rock.

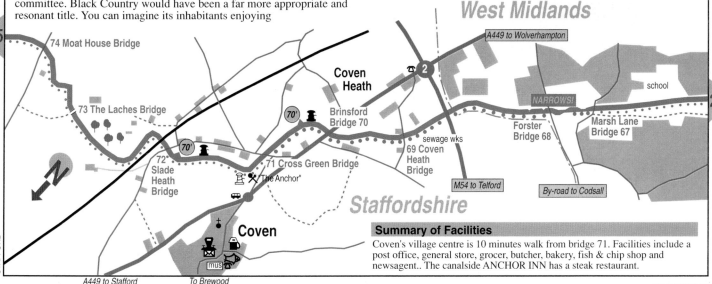

Summary of Facilities

Coven's village centre is 10 minutes walk from bridge 71. Facilities include a post office, general store, grocer, butcher, bakery, fish & chip shop and newsagent.. The canalside ANCHOR INN has a steak restaurant.

SHROPSHIRE UNION

Avenue Bridge No.10, evokes the mysterious atmosphere of the old Birmingham & Liverpool Junction Canal

DESPITE the proximity of Wolverhampton, Autherley, like many canal junctions, is self-contained; though it is not pretty in a conventional sense, being bordered by housing estates, sewage plants and public open spaces. Travellers on the FOUR COUNTIES RING exchange the Staffordshire & Worcestershire Canal for the Shropshire Union here, or vice versa, and the urban fringe of Wolverhampton amounts to little more than a brief interruption whatever your direction of travel. Half a mile south of Autherley lies Aldersley Junction, turnstile to the esoteric charms of the Birmingham Canal Navigations. Stick southbound to the Staffs & Worcs, and in thirteen hours you can be in Stourport-on-Severn. Decisions, decisions!

The old boatmen called Autherley "Cut End" for the obvious reason that the Shropshire Union Canal began and ended here. Once there was all the paraphernalia of a meeting of the waterways: toll office, stables, workshops, employees cottages, and a dominant, sweeping roving bridge carrying the Staffordshire & Worcestershire Canal's towpath over the entrance to the Shropshire Union. A stop lock - just six inches deep - protected the two companies' precious water supplies. Much of this infastructure survives, enjoying a new lease of life in the leisure age as a hire base and boatyard.

A massive sewage works provides the canal with much of its water supply; suitably treated of course, or perhaps this explains the Shropshire Union's apparent impatience to get on with its journey to the north-west. Whatever the motivation, Autherley is quickly forgotten as the canal crosses the boundary between West Midlands and Staffordshire and leaves the housing estates of suburban Wolverhampton behind. The land east of the canal was once occupied by an aerodrome, whilst the works by bridge 4 was formerly an aircraft factory, turning out, amongst other designs, the 'Defiant' fighter plane.

An 'invisible' aqueduct carries the canal over the little River Penk before the waterway goes through a series of contortions which see it narrowing, then widening, then narrowing again before resuming its usual width beyond bridge 6. The M54 introduces a moment of twentieth century reality, but otherwise the landscape is peacefully rural, setting the scene of the forty mile journey to Nantwich through some unexpectedly remote countryside.

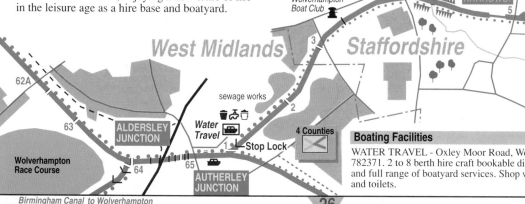

Boating Facilities

WATER TRAVEL - Oxley Moor Road, Wolverhampton WV9 5HW. Tel: 01902 782371. 2 to 8 berth hire craft bookable direct or through Hoseasons. Pumpout, and full range of boatyard services. Shop with souvenirs and groceries, payphone and toilets.

THE Shropshire Union slices through the Staffordshire countryside in cuttings and upon embankments typical of the bold, 19th century designs of Thomas Telford, who engineered this route between Autherley and Nantwich, originally known as the Birmingham & Liverpool Junction Canal. Travelling northwards you rapidly become attuned to the unique atmosphere of this canal. Far from becoming monotonous, its purposeful, loping stride across the landscape seems to engender a strange exhilarance, intensified by the recurring contrast of shadowy cuttings and panorama providing embankments, known as 'rockings' and 'valleys' respectively to past generations of boatmen.

There are two notable structures either side of Brewood. To the south the distinctly ornate, balustraded Avenue Bridge (No.10) carries the

carriageway to Chillington Hall. The advent of the canals heralded many similar attempts at ornamentation and disguise, where powerful landowners would only condescend to permit a waterway to cross their parklands if suitable steps were taken to adorn the otherwise purely functional architecture of the new trade route. In contrast, north of Brewood, the canal crosses the old Roman Road of Watling Street on a sturdy, yet elegant aqueduct of iron, brick and stone construction. Canal travellers, be they on foot (the towpath here being part of the "Staffordshire Way") or afloat, can gaze down with a very real sense of superiority on the traffic of the A5, in full knowledge that their's is the older, wiser mode of transport. Belvide Reservoir is one of the main sources of water supply for the Shropshire Union Canal. Broom Hall was the home of William Carlos who hid King Charles II in the oak tree at nearby Boscobel after the Battle of Worcester in 1651.

Brewood

A lovely village, retaining an ancient air of calm. The natives call it "Brood", and there really is a timelessness about it which seduces you into spending longer here than you might have planned. Winding lanes of gracious houses lead to the old market place where the archaic vehicles of the Green Bus Company pause before rumbling off to Wolverhampton. Enhancing one corner of the square is "Speedwell Castle", a Gothick fantasy erected in the 18th century on the winnings of a racehorse called Speedwell. Within cycling distance to the west lies Boscobel House where Charles II was hidden in an oak tree.

Eating & Drinking

ADMIRAL RODNEY - Church Street. Effectively refurbished by the Black Country brewers Holt, Plant & Deakin in Victorian parlour style. Good bar meals, families catered for. Garden with playground. Several other pubs as well.

Shopping

Old fashioned shops where you can eavesdrop on local gossip: baker, butcher, chemist, newsagent with post office counter, small supermarket and branch of Lloyds Bank. Calor gas from garage by bridge 14.

Public Transport

BUSES - splendid Green Bus Co services on an hourly basis (Mon-Sat) to/from Wolverhampton. some run through to/from Wheaton Aston and are thus useful for one-way towpath walks. Tel: Cheslyn Hay 01922 414141.

Boating Facilities

COUNTRYWIDE CRUISERS - Brewood, Staffs ST19 9BG. Tel: 01902 850166. 4 - 8 berth hire craft. Pumpout, small shop selling gifts and chandlery and all the usual boatyard services. Blue Riband Club members.

WHEATON ASTON Lock is strangely solitary - the only one in 25 miles of canal; a telling statistic of Telford's engineering. For about a mile the canal penetrates the deciduous heart of Lapley Wood, and there's another typical Shroppie cutting by Little Onn, but elsewhere the embankments offer wide views eastwards towards Cannock Chase.

How astonishingly remote and unpeopled the landscape seems. The West Midlands conurbation is less than a dozen miles to the south, yet moor for the night between Wheaton Aston and Little Onn, and you'll have only the occasional eerie hoot of a hunting owl, or the distant silent wash of headlights on a country lane, for company.

Abandoned wartime aerodromes inevitably have their ghosts, and in decay accumulate a patina of lore and legend, hard perhaps to equate with the often mundane use to which they were put after closure. Wheaton Aston was opened in 1941 and became one of the RAF's largest training units, operating a squadron of 'Oxfords'. It was by all accounts an unenviable posting, there being little in the way of entertainment for off-duty pilots and ground staff. There were however occasional dramas. Once an American 'Thunderbolt' crash-landed in the canal. Another well remembered wartime incident occurred at the lock when a narrowboat, carrying an unsheeted cargo of shining aluminium on a moonlit night, was attacked by a German aircraft which unleashed a bomb that exploded less than a hundred yards from the chamber. Swords into ploughshares: after the war the aerodrome became a pig farm!

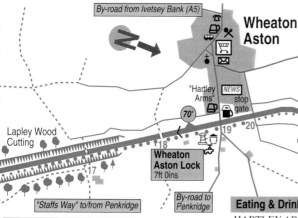

Wheaton Aston

Dormitory housing has suffocated the original village, but people have to live somewhere, and the 'incomers' natter on their way to and from the shops much as the farmwives would have done when Wheaton Aston was solely a farming community. No, this is no picture postcard village, but after its late twentieth century fashion it's a village alive and kicking, and therefore arguably more justifiable than a village pretty but pickled.

Eating & Drinking

HARTLEY ARMS - canalside bridge 19. Comfortable refurbished canal pub offering a wide range of food and Banks's ales.
LA CALVADOS - strange to find a thriving French restaurant in a village like this. Open Tue-Sat for dinner and on Sunday lunch. Tel: 01785 840707 for bookings. Slightly pricey.

Shopping

Post office, general stores, baker, butchers, newsagents and grocers all within 5 minutes walk of bridge 19. Most shops slumber at lunchtime. Turner's canalside garage stocks Calor gas, very cheap diesel and boating accessories.

Public Transport

BUSES - regular but not frequent services to/from Brewood, Wolverhampton, Penkridge and Cannock. Tel: 01543 577099

DEEP shadowy sandstone cuttings, spanned by lichened grey stone bridges of simple balance and unaffected beauty, lead to the eighty-one unlined yards of Cowley Tunnel; the only one on the Shropshire Union. Once a dizzy jungle of trees darkened the approaches so much that you were never quite sure where the tunnel began and the cutting ended, but their roots caused instabilities in what was already a brittle rock strata (Telford, and his contractor William Provis, had intended the tunnel to be much longer) and they were felled in 1985, leaving the cutting strangely bare to those who had known it before. The buildings of two wharves remain

intact at High Onn. One belonged to Cadburys, the other to a local landowner, hinting at a degree of agricultural traffic on the canal. Nearby lies St Editha's Well whose waters are reputed to cure poor eyesight, but we couldn't see it.

On a clear day the embankments north of Gnosall reveal that famous Shropshire landmark, The Wrekin, 15 miles to the south-west; a slumbering hunchback of a summit, 1335ft high. A.E. Housman immortalised it in "A Shropshire Lad", and Salopians raise their glasses "To all friends around the Wrekin."

The dismantled railway line which crossed the canal at Gnosall once usefully connected Stafford with Shrewsbury until a certain doctor made his presence felt. Historically it was unusual in that it was actually built by the Shropshire Union Canal Company, apparently hedging their bets on the transport mode of the future. When, in 1846, they leased themselves to the London & North Western Railway, few shareholders would have backed the canal to outlast the railway as it has done.

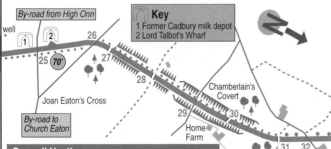

Key
1 Former Cadbury milk depot
2 Lord Talbot's Wharf

Gnosall Heath

This appendage of Gnosall (No-zull) grew up with the coming of the canal. Two pubs slaked the thirst of passing boatmen, a steam powered flour mill took advantage of the new transport mode, and a non-conformist chapel kept a sense of proportion amidst all the excitement. Nowadays the pubs pander to pleasure boaters and passing motorists, the flour mill has become a private residence, and the chapel is a hardware store. Gnosall itself lies half a mile or so to the east; pleasant enough, but hardly compelling unless you have an enthusiasm for ecclesiastical architecture, for the parish church is substantial and largely 13th century.

Eating & Drinking

THE BOAT - bridge 34. Well known canal pub with curiously attractive curved wall abutting the bridge. Marston's, bar food, bar billiards and pleasant garden by the water's edge.
THE NAVIGATION - bridge 35. Wards ales (a

long way from Sheffield!) lunches and garden with good children's playground.
Fish & chips on A518 open daily ex Sun both sessions.

Shopping

General store, newsagent and butcher by bridge 34, plus bakery further along Wharf Road towards Gnosall. Post office by bridge 35.

Public Transport

BUSES - Midland Red to/from Stafford & Newport, Tel:01543 577099.

A MASK of tall trees disguises the immensity of Shelmore embankment. It was six years in the making and, in its way, was as glorious an engineering feat as any of Telford's more visibly imposing aqueducts. A vast army of navvies and horses was employed on it. Spoil from the big cuttings at nearby Gnosall and Grub Street was brought by wagon for its construction. To Telford's dismay the earthworks slipped time after time and, as the rest of the canal was finished, Shelmore stubbornly refused to hold. In poor health, Telford struggled to oversee its completion, conscious that the bank need not have been tackled at all, had Lord Anson of Norbury Park sanctioned the preferred course through Shelmore Wood. Perhaps we should regard his lordship more kindly from the perspective of the twentieth century where environmentalists, protecting the landscape from the intrusion of new motorways, are deemed to be on the side of the angels.

Sadly, Norbury is no longer a juncton, though the name lives on. How nice it would be now to lock down the 'Seventeen Steps' of the Newport Branch and head across the marshy emptiness of Shropshire's Weald Moors to Shrewsbury, encountering Telford's early cast iron aqueduct at Longdon-on-Tern and the 970 yards of Berwick Tunnel. We can but dream, for though some attempts were made in the Sixties and Seventies to restore the canal, they proved fruitless.

North of Norbury lies Grub Street cutting. For over a mile the canal is wrapped in a thick coat of vegetation, again, like Shelmore, hiding the sheer size of the eighty feet deep cutting. A ruined landing stage recalls the extraction of clay for the canal bed, but the cutting's most unusual feature is the double-arched bridge which carries the A519 across the canal. The tiny telegraph pole is a survivor from the line which once marched beside the Shroppie for much of its length. Ironically canals are being used again as lines of communication with the burying of optical fibres beneath selected lengths of towpath. A black, monkey-like creature is reputed to have haunted bridge 39 ever since a boatman was killed here in the 19th century.

Course of Newport Branch Canal

NORBURY JUNCTION

Shelmore Embankment

"Junction Inn"

Norbury

70'

BW

38

Shropshire Union Cruises

A519 from Newport

"The Anchor"

42 · 43

39

Grub Street Cutting

41

40

By-road to High Offley

A519 to Eccleshall

32

Norbury Junction

Though the suffix is misleading nowadays, Norbury remains a flourishing canal centre where British Waterways have an office and maintenance yard. One or two of the houses are still occupied by canal workers, but three are available for holiday let through the boatyard. Indeed, Norbury attracts land-based visitors like a magnet and, mindful of their potential as boating holidaymakers, the local hire base operates day and trip boat services to whet the appetite for canal cruises of lengthier duration.

Eating & Drinking

THE MEASHAM TEAPOT - cosy little adjunct to the boatyard shop. Light meals and refreshments usually available during the cruising season.

JUNCTION INN - canalside bridge 38. Busy but not brash pub with lots of facilities. Garden with children's play area. Bar and restaurant meals.
ANCHOR INN - canalside bridge 42. Delightfully unspoilt boatman's pub. Various 'real ales' including Manchester brewed Oak bitter served fresh from the barrel in the cellar. One of a vanishing breed.

Boating Facilities

SHROPSHIRE UNION CRUISES - Norbury Junction, Stafford ST20 0PN. Tel: 01785 284292. 2 - 12 berth hire craft bookable through Dartline (01829 260638) or Blakes. Pumpout, gift shop, groceries and payphone plus all the usual boatyard facilities. Dayboat hire and holiday cottages to let.

CROSSING the border between Staffordshire and Shropshire, the canal continues to traverse an uncluttered countryside almost entirely given over to agriculture. It can come as a surprise to find so remote a landscape in the 'crowded' middle of England. One is tempted to categorise the area as 'lost' but for the obvious truth that it has never been 'found' in the first place. Country roads, largely innocent of traffic, cross the canal but rarely run parallel to it, defying easy exploration of "The Shroppie" in a motor car.

Blithely we pleasure boaters sail across the Shroppie's embankments and through its cuttings with no more thought for their construction than if we were driving down the M6. But imagine the impact of Telford's brash new canal on the surrounding early nineteenth century landscape. Put yourself in the position of Sir Richard Whitworth's tenant farmer at Batchacre Park. Up until 1830 dawn rose across the open pasturelands throwing light through his east-facing windows. A year later his view of the rising sun was cut off forever by an embankment twice the height of the farmhouse. No wonder the landowners of this rural corner of Staffordshire had their misgivings, and the canal company paid dearly in compensation for the land they acquired.

At Knighton one comes suddenly upon a disconcertingly large factory. It seems intrusive amidst these rolling pastures until you discover that it was opened by Cadburys, the chocolate manufacturers, in 1911 as a centre for processing milk collected from the dairy farming hinterland of the Shropshire Union Canal. Canal transport was used exclusively to bring countless churns gathered from numerous wharves along the canal; from simple wooden stages at the foot of fields, to the sophistication of Cadbury's own plant at High Onn. Cadburys owned a distinctive fleet of narrowboats, being one of the first operators to experiment with motorised craft. Cocoa and sugar crumb were also brought by boat to Knighton and blended with milk to make raw chocolate, itself returned to Bournville, again by boat, to be transformed into the finished delicacy.

The last boatman to trade to Knighton was Charlie Atkins senior; nicknamed 'Chocolate Charlie' for obvious reasons. He carried the final cargo from Knighton to Bournville in 1961. Since then all transport to and from the still busy works has been by road. Attempts to have the handsome Art Deco type canalside buildings demolished have been staved off by a preservation order, though unless some new use is found disintegration will undoubtedly ensue.

Beyond Knighton Wood lie the remains of Knighton Reservoir. It tried manfully to supply water to the canal despite seepage through the underlying rock strata. Now it is the haunt of fishermen and wildfowl. Good views of The Wrekin are to be had in the vicinity of Park Heath and Little Soudley.

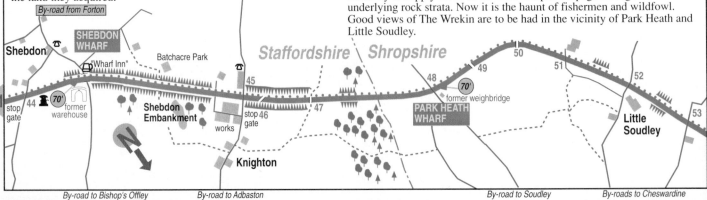

THE Shroppie flirts with the county boundary, the towpath forming the demarcation so that, technically, the canal lies briefly in Staffordshire. The landscape, though, is impervious to the machinations of local government, remaining aloof and typically remote: a tall, dark, silent canal, this Shropshire Union.

WOODSEAVES is another prodigious cutting. The canal narrows and, in places, is cut through solid rock. These cuttings proved just as troublesome to Telford and his contractors as did the embankments. There were frequent avalanches during construction and, even today, brittle lumps of sandstone are inclined to dislodge themselves and tumble into the canal; one reason why a 2mph speed limit is imposed. A feature of Woodseaves is its pair of high bridges, spanning the canal like portals to the mysterious chasms of another world.

At TYRLEY a flight of five locks - the last to be faced southbound for seventeen miles - carries the canal down into, or up out of, Market Drayton. The lower chambers are located in a shadowy sandstone cutting across which branches intertwine to form a tunnel of trees. Damp and rarely touched by sunlight, all manner of mosses and ferns flourish in this conducive environment. After dusk bats leave their tree bole roosts to hunt for insects, acrobatically twisting and turning over the luminous pounds between the locks. The well surfaced towpath makes the flight popular with pedestrians

but parking is restricted on the lane which crosses the canal by bridge 60. The provision of a sanitary station and rubbish point above the top lock satisfies the need of boaters too.

TYRLEY WHARF was a point of discharge and collection for the local estate at Peatswood. The buildings date from 1837 and were erected in a graceful Tudor style by the local landowner. Nowadays, its commercial significance a thing of the dim and distant past, it would be difficult to imagine a more picturesque scene, though it is sad that the craft shop and home-baking outlet, admirable enterprises of the 1980s, have both been and gone. At least four crafts shops have flourished, then perished, in the thirteen years of our Canal Companion researches, and we sense a marked lack of new enterprise and energy on the canals in general as we move towards the end of the century.

Summary of Facilities

There are no shops to be found on this length of canal other than by walking a country mile from Goldstone Wharf to Cheswardine; though with names as beautiful as that you could spend the walking time turning a verse or two. THE WHARF TAVERN (bridge 55) is one of 'The Shroppie's' most popular pubs, widely regarded for its restaurant meals. Bar food - including an ample summer buffet - is also readily available. There's a spacious canalside garden and a payphone on the premises. Half a mile west of Tyrley top lock the lane joins the main road at THE FOUR ALLS, one of the new breed of 'open all day' inns.

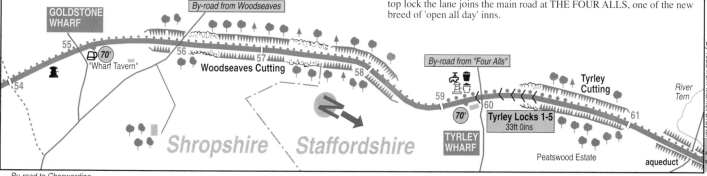

GOLDSTONE WHARF · By-road from Woodseaves · 55 · "Wharf Tavern" (70') · 56 · 57 · Woodseaves Cutting · 58 · By-road from "Four Alls" · 59 · 60 · Tyrley Cutting · 61 · River Tern · By-road from Market Drayton · Shropshire · Staffordshire · TYRLEY WHARF · Tyrley Locks 1-5 33ft 0ins · (70') · Peatswood Estate · aqueduct · 54 · 2 · 34 · By-road to Cheswardine

MARKET DRAYTON was the largest, in fact the only town encountered by the old Birmingham & Liverpool Junction Canal on its route from Autherley to Nantwich. Not surprisingly a sizeable wharf was provided for dealing with local cargoes; though the canal's monopoly on local trade lasted only thirty years before the railway reached the town. It is sometimes difficult, in these days of the ubiquitous juggernaut, to appreciate the importance of the canal wharf and the railway goods yard to the past prosperity of small towns like Drayton. They must have been the hub of local life, few businesses would have been able to carry out their trade without regular recourse to the wharfinger and the stationmaster. From the opening of the canal until the First World War no commodity, apart from local agricultural produce, could have arrived at Market Drayton, or been dispatched, without the involvement of these important gentlemen. On the canal a large basin and a sizeable warehouse and adjoining cornmill remind us of this lost significance. The buildings are beautiful in their own right and deserve to have a use found for them, having lain empty and disused for many years.

Pleasant 48 hour moorings, bordered by school playing fields, stretch south from bridge 62 to the imposing aqueduct over the by-road to Peatswood.

Steps lead down to the road below, which crosses the little River Tern nearby and forms the most romantic, but not the most convenient, approach to the town centre.

BETTON CUTTING is not among 'The Shroppie's' most dramatic, but it is reputed to be haunted by a shrieking spectre, and working boatmen would avoid lingering here in the old days. Indeed, it could be said that this whole canal has something of a fey quality about it, a blurring of past and present which is liable to send shivers down susceptible spines.

ADDERLEY LOCKS used to win prizes for being particularly beautiful and well maintained, but British Waterways have moved away from the practice of appointing full time lock-keepers to individual flights and Adderley, though neat enough, is not the place it was when every chamber was bordered by flower beds and the grass manicured like a bowling green. A privet hedge beside the third lock down betrays the site of a demolished lock-keeper's cottage. A great number of these vanished from the canal system in the Fifties and Sixties as trade diminished past the point of no return. A sad loss, though one can sympathise with cash-strapped British Waterways's reluctance to fund their upkeep, let alone their rateable value, on an indefinite basis.

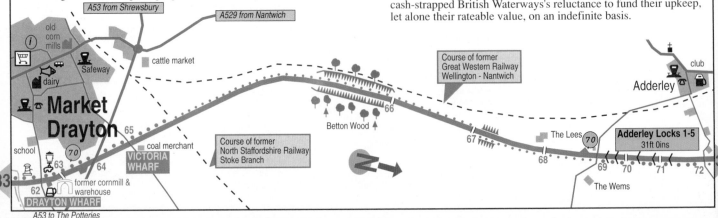

Tyrley Locks

Market Drayton

Self-styled as "The Home of Gingerbread", the day to see Drayton at its best is Wednesday when the 750 years old market still packs the quaint, narrow streets with stalls and country bumpkins intent on a bargain and a gossip. This gregarious gathering is the town's real heritage, along with its half-timbered town houses which mostly date from the aftermath of a fire which swept the place in 1651. Drayton's most famous son was Robert Clive. By all accounts he couldn't wait to get away. He is best remembered here for scaling the sturdy tower of St Mary's and blackmailing local shopkeepers. Such youthful escapades were ideal preparation for a career in diplomacy and military leadership. He established British rule in the sub-continent and became known as 'Clive of India'.

Eating & Drinking

Drayton bristles with pubs and Marston's beer seems to predominate. Nearest the canal, THE TALBOT, is a handsome, redbrick Georgian inn just east of bridge 62. On the walk into town the LAMB HOTEL can be recommended for meals and THE STAR for its Wem brewed Hanby Ales. In the centre the CORBET ARMS is an old coaching inn offering morning coffees, lunches, teas and dinners.

Shopping

Wednesdays, and to a lesser extent, Saturdays are market day. Browsing from stall to stall you'll find the meat and dairy outlets particularly good. BROWNS in the High Street is an old fashioned provision merchant specialising in local produce, Potteries oatcakes and pikelets and Billingtons gingerbread. There are branches of all the main banks, a launderette in Shropshire Street, and a Safeway supermarket near the old railway station.

Public Transport

BUSES - PMT/Midland Red to/from Stoke and Shrewsbury. One or two buses on market day operate to/from Audlem providing a useful link for towpath walkers. Tel: 01952 291300

FIFTEEN locks running through a cutting of larch and Scots pine take the canal across the Shropshire/Cheshire border. The locks are well-maintained and a pleasure to operate. The lock-keeper at the top of the flight used to hire out horses to help butty boats up and down the locks. The barrel-roofed building by lock 10 was used by stonemasons, blacksmiths and carpenters engaged in maintaining the flight. Towards the foot of the flight - known to old boatmen as the Audlem "Thick" - you pass Audlem Wharf, one of the prettiest ports of call on the Shropshire Union, with a former warehouse restored as a popular pub and the adjacent lofty mill converted into a superb craft shop.

North of the bottom lock, below which is a well preserved stable block used as a base by the Daystar Theatre Group, the canal, wide with concrete banking but deceptively shallow, bounds across the infant River Weaver on a high embankment. One of the craziest notions of the Ministry of War Transport during World War II was to make the Weaver navigable by 100 ton barges to this point, beyond which a lift would carry them up to the level of the Shropshire Union, upgraded sufficiently for them to travel as far south as Wolverhampton. Pleasure boaters can be thankful that this scheme never got off the drawing board, but there are those of us who do believe that inland waterways, properly invested in, could have a role to play in the safe, environmentally harmonious, carriage of heavy goods.

Swanbach
Coxbank
Pool House
Kinsell Farm
Cheshire
Shropshire
A529
A525 from Whitchurch
70'
aqueduct
80
River Weaver
Moss Hall
Audlem Mill
Hankelow Mill
Audlem Locks 1-15
93ft 0ins
Audlem
A525 to Newcastle
A529 to Nantwich

Audlem

"The sleepers sleep at Audlem" sang Flanders and Swann in "Slow Train", their elegy for the Beeching cuts, and whilst they were referring to the village's station and its imminent closure, Audlem remains a sleepy sort of place, rarely mentioned in guidebooks. Now that the trains have gone and the average motorist is hell bent on getting somewhere else as fast as he can, only the canal traveller is journeying at a pace to do this lovely village justice.

Eating & Drinking

THE BRIDGE - canalside bridge 78. Unspoilt former boatman's pub serving Marston's and a good choice of food.

THE SHROPPIE FLY - canalside lock 13. Warehouse conversion with bar formed from an old narrowboat. Bar and restaurant meals.
THE LORD COMBERMERE - The Square. Popular village local. Food, families welcome.
MADDOCKS - fish & chips and Wrights pies. "Maddocks for Haddocks!"
OLD PRIESTS HOUSE - The Square. Coffees, teas and light lunches.
PIZZA PARLOUR - Little Italy comes to Cheshire!

Public Transport

BUSES - services to/from Nantwich (Mon-Sat) and Market Drayton (Weds). Both useful for one-way towpath walks. Tel: 01270 505350.

Shopping

Friendly shops cater for most needs and make shopping here a pleasure rather than a stressful chore. Most shops indulge in a lunchtime siesta, though, and Wednesday is half-day. Ice cream, made on the premises, is available from the old fashioned confectioners by the market cross. Audlem's outstanding establishment, however, is the AUDLEM MILL CANAL SHOP converted from the three-storey Kingbur mill by John Stothert in 1976. Shopping and browsing here is, in the proprietor's own words: "More a social event than a retail experience."

A T Hack Green there are two isolated locks and the remnants of a stable, recalling the practice of frequent changes of horses on the 'fly' boats which travelled day and night with urgent, perishable cargoes. This is the Cheshire Plain and dairy farming has long been a vital part of the area's economy. We tend to think of farming as an unchanging facet of the landscape, but the Fresian cattle so synonymous with the county are a relatively recent introduction. The working boatman of the 19th century would not recognise these black & white interlopers from the Low Countries. When he passed this way the pastures would have been grazed by indigenous breeds like Ayrshires and Alderneys.

The Birmingham & Liverpool Junction Canal was opened between Autherley and Nantwich in 1835 - the last major canal, other than the Manchester Ship Canal which was in a different league altogether, to be built in Britain. By the time it was opened, however, the canal promoters and builders had been overtaken by the Railway Age. Narrowboats carrying 25 tons at an average speed of 3mph were no competition for goods trains steaming along at 25mph trailing several hundred tons behind them. Nevertheless, after it was taken over by the London & North Western Railway in 1846,

the Shropshire Union Canal continued to be well used, largely because it penetrated rival Great Western Railway territory, and there was a good deal of competition for cargoes.

In fact, commercial trade survived on this canal until the 1960s, which must be some sort of testimony to the viability of canal carrying. Perhaps in the final analysis attitudes rather than economics prevailed. One of the most celebrated traffics on the Shroppie in latter years was Thomas Clayton's oil run from Stanlow, on the banks of the Mersey, to Langley Green, near Oldbury in the Black Country. The contract commenced in 1924 and the Clayton boats, with their characteristic decked holds, and bearing names of rivers, were a mainstay of trade on the canal for thirty years. Even post-war, a thousand boat-loads per annum were being dispatched from Stanlow, some remaining horse-drawn until the early Fifties. But, in common with other narrow canals, the Shropshire Union lost its final freights to the motor lorry, and, for many, with the disappearance of its working boats, something died on the Shroppie; some intangible component of canal heritage that no amount of preservation, nor hectic holiday trade, can compensate for.

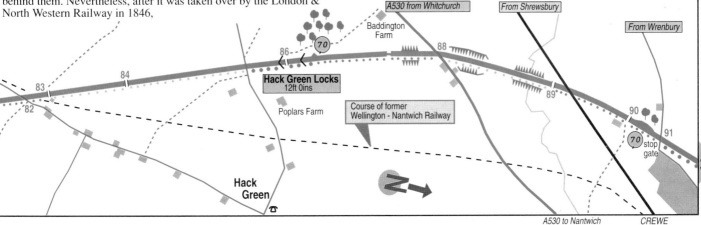

A530 from Whitchurch

From Shrewsbury

From Wrenbury

Baddington Farm

86 · · · 70

84

88

83

82

Hack Green Locks
12ft 0ins

Poplars Farm

89

90

91

70 stop gate

Course of former
Wellington - Nantwich Railway

N →

Hack Green

37

A530 to Nantwich

CREWE

*T*HE character of the Shropshire Union Canal changes perceptibly at Nantwich: northwards lie the broad, winding waters of its earlier constituent, the Chester Canal; southwards the direct and narrow Birmingham & Liverpool Junction Canal. A broad embankment elevates the canal above the housing, back gardens and allotments which constitute the periphery of Nantwich. Ironically, these earthworks, together with a cast iron aqueduct over the Chester road, could have been avoided if the owners of Dorfold Hall had not objected to the passage of the canal across their land. The basin and former terminus of the Chester Canal indicates the more expedient route to the south which Telford would have liked to have used. Nowadays it provides valuable mooring space, long and short term, and there is a certain pleasure to be had from manouevering in and out of its narrow confines. Correspondent Anthony Macdonald Smith drew our attention to the notice at Henhull Moorings stating that "Priority is given to those wishing to moor." It means, he interprets, that those who don't want to moor must not moor out of spite in order to prevent those who want to moor from doing so!

Nantwich

The octagonal tower of St Mary's church, glimpsed across the rooftops from the high canal embankment, tempts you to moor and get to know this picturesque and historic Cheshire town. Walking in from the basin, the aqueduct forms an appropriate portcullis, and the appeal of the town increases as the centre is reached. Few English towns are cleaner or better endowed with floral displays. In medieval times Nantwich was the chief salt producing town in the county. For a brief Victorian heyday it flourished as a spa town.

Eating & Drinking

No shortage here of tearooms, coaching inns or ethnic restaurants, though all are at least 15 minutes walk in from the canal. On this occasion we'll leave you to your own devices. The nearest pub, THE ODDFELLOWS ARMS on Welsh Row, is little over 5 minutes away, however, and it's a pleasant Burtonwood house offering home made cooking. Families are catered for.

Public Transport

BUSES - services throughout area. The Hanley - Chester service C84 calls at Barbridge . TRAINS - services to/from Crewe and Shrewsbury. Tel: 01782 411411.

Shopping

There is a Home Counties air of affluence about the shops of Nantwich. There are antique shops and boutiques by the dozen, but what is most satisfying is the sheer quality of the food sellers: butchers like CLEWLOWS and bakers like CHATWINS, both of whom have branches in Pepper Street. A market is held on Thursdays and Saturdays, whilst Wednesdays are half-days. The marina shop stocks a selection of provisions, and there is also an excellent corner shop on the corner of the Wrenbury road, easily reached from the aqueduct .

Places to Visit

TOURIST INFORMATION - Beam Street (by bus station). Tel: 01270 623914.
NANTWICH MUSEUM - Pillory Street..
Interesting displays of local history; salt, cheese etc. Tel: 01270 627104.

Boating Facilities

SOUTH SHORE NARROWBOATS - Chester Road, Nantwich CW5 8LB. Tel: 01270 625122..
Pumpout, moorings, shop with groceries, gifts and chandlery and full range of boating services.
SIMOLDA - Basin End, Nantwich CW5 8LA. Tel: 01270 624075. 3 to 8 berth hire craft.

HURLESTON and Barbridge are the 'Clapham Junctions' of the inland waterways. Throughout the cruising season the section between them is often frenetic with boats converging and diverging to and from all points of the canal compass. Providentially the old Chester Canal (opened in 1779) was built to barge dimensions and there is usually plenty of room to manoeuvre. The Cheshire Plain's recurring image of spacious pastures grazed by Fresian cattle continues unabated; come milking time the herds shuffle udder-heavy across the accommodation bridges of the canal.

HURLESTON JUNCTION, with its quartet of locks, is the starting point of the Llangollen Canal's serene journey into Wales; a route fully covered in our "Shropshire Union Canal Companion." It's overlooked by a high-banked reservoir which receives its water supplies from the Llangollen Canal, a factor instrumental in the survival of the waterway back in 1944 when there were proposals to close it.

BARBRIDGE JUNCTION marks the beginning and end of the Middlewich Branch of the Shropshire Union Canal, and it is, along with Middlewich, Great Haywood and Autherley, a pivotal point for all Four Counties Ring travellers. On this map we include the length of canal up to Bunbury simply for the benefit of boaters journeying to or from the boatyard there. Barbridge is an incredibly popular overnight mooring spot, and it pays to get here early at the height of the season to be sure of a place. The main road apart, it is easy to see its attraction, with two canalside pubs vying for custom and the interest of the juncton itself, where once a transhipment shed spanned the main line. You can detect its site where the canal narrows just south of the junction.

Summary of Facilities

Both the BARBRIDGE INN (bridge 100) and the JOLLY TAR (opposite junction) cater for families and offer a wide choice of food and nice big gardens where any children in your party can let off steam. Just beneath the embankment at Barbridge Junction the POST OFFICE STORES deals in canal souvenirs. Note also the FARM SHOP on the A51 adjacent to Hurleston top lock. BUSES run hourly from stops at Wardle linking Chester and Hanley via Nantwich. Details on Crewe 01270 505350.

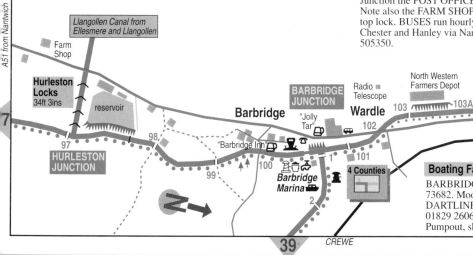

Boating Facilities

BARBRIDGE MARINA - Wardle, Nantwich CW5 6BE Tel: 01270 73682. Moorings, gas, repairs, slipway, boatbuilding, chandlery etc.
DARTLINE - Bunbury Wharf, Tarporley, Cheshire CW6 9QB. Tel: 01829 260638. 2 to 12 berth hire craft (Blakes). Day boat hire. Pumpout, shop, full range of services.

REMOTE, and seemingly always windswept, the Middlewich Branch of the Shropshire Union cuts across the grain of the landscape on a series of high embankments. For all its loneliness, though, it can be a busy length of canal because, as well as Four Counties Ring traffic, it funnels boats to and from the hugely popular Llangollen Canal, consequently its four deep and heavy-gated locks can become bottlenecks at the beginning and end of summer weeks.

Historically, the branch, opened in 1833, belonged to the Chester Canal Company and was engineered by Thomas Telford. Trade was heavy in cargo-carrying days, as after opening of the Birmingham & Liverpool Junction Canal this became the optimum route between the Black Country and the industrial North-west. Trade also developed between Ellesmere Port on the banks of the Mersey and The Potteries: Cornish china clay in one direction finished crockery in the other. In 1888 a curious experiment was undertaken to see if it was feasible to replace horse-power, by laying a narrow gauge railway along the towpath below Cholmondeston Lock, and employing a small steam locomotive called "Dickie" to haul strings of narrowboats. The concept didn't develop here, laying the track was considered cost-prohibitive and there were problems in steering the boats, though it did catch on abroad, especially on the French waterways.

Cholmondeston still retains a railway presence, however, in the shape of the Crewe to Chester railway, part of the historic route of the "Irish Mails" to Holyhead, a line regularly used by steam-hauled specials.

A high, wooded embankment carries the canal across the River Weaver. Four Counties Ring travellers meet the river again near Audlem. It rises on the south-facing slopes of the Peckforton Hills, passes beneath the Llangollen Canal at Wrenbury prior to becoming navigable at Winsford, less than five miles downstream of the Weaver Aqueduct. There is nothing spectacular about the canal's crossing of the river, but it takes place in the most agreeable of locations and, passing on your elevated way, it's hard to escape a fleeting sense of regret that the riverbank, being on private land, cannot so easily be explored. A yearning, one suspects, for the unattainable: like the girl at the bus stop who you pass each day but will never get to know, or the job that you suspect you could do brilliantly but are unlikely to be ever offered.

Boating Facilities

VENETIAN MARINE - Cholmondeston, Nantwich, Cheshire CW5 6DD. Tel: 01270 528318 & 528251. Extensive 'marina village' offering moorings, sales, chandlery, repairs and a wide range of other boating facilities. Provisions, crafts and tea rooms.

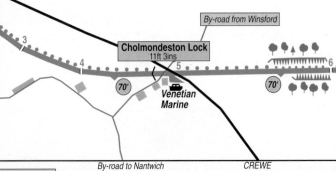

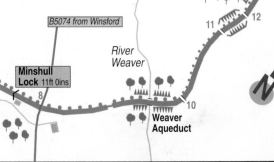

TO subconsciously relegate the Middlewich Branch to the back of your mind as an unspectacular, but necessary link in the waterways of the North-west would be unjust, for this is a rumbustious canal, extrovertly ushering you loftily above the snaking valley of the Weaver, presenting you with expansive views towards a horizon bounded by Delamere Forest and the Peckforton Hills. Church Minshull - all russet coloured brick and black & white half timbering - looks wistfully, from the canal's elevated position, like a toy vilage embracing the river's luxuriant banks. Tom and Angela Rolt enjoyed an extended stay here in the fateful Autumn of 1939 while Tom worked for Rolls Royce at Crewe. It was tedious work he didn't enjoy, but the couple revelled in the close-knit community which flourished at Minshull: the blacksmith who shod the local cart horses; and the miller whose water wheels supplied the village with its electricity, continuing to do so right up until 1960.

Several sizeable farms border the canal, their fields filled with black & white milking herds or cut red by the plough in a ruddy shade of corduroy.

Some old canal horse stables stand adjacent to bridge 18. Near bridge 22 woods hide the Top Flash, a subsidence induced lake beside the Weaver. The main London-Glasgow railway crosses the canal, its sleek electric trains swishing by at thirty times the speed of your boat, but as we have noted elsewhere, the essence of real travel has no corollary with velocity. To the south-east lies a forgotten, older transport route, a Roman road which linked the early salt mines at Nantwich and Middlewich.

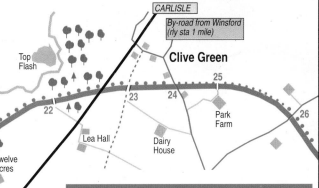

CARLISLE

By-road from Winsford (rly sta 1 mile)

Clive Green

Top Flash

25

23 24

22

Park Farm

26

Lea Hall

Dairy House

21

Twelve Acres

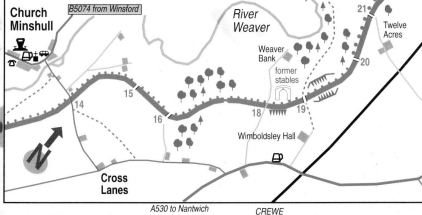

Church Minshull

B5074 from Winsford

River Weaver

Weaver Bank

former stables

20

15

14

16

18

19

Wimboldsley Hall

N

Cross Lanes

A530 to Nantwich

CREWE

Church Minshull

A peaceful, pretty village of black & white cottages. Bridge 14 seems to be a popular overnight mooring spot, though the inhabitants of the old wharf house don't like you to moor in front of their windows; and can you blame them? THE BADGER is an historic pub located in the village centre. Les Routiers recommended, it offers bar and restaurant meals, a garden and a games room. A small POST OFFICE STORES lurks behind the pub and doubles as an off licence and newsagents too. It closes early on Wednesdays but does open on Sunday mornings. BUSES operate hourly Mon-Sat connecting with Crewe and Northwich (Tel: 01270 505350).

CALDON
CANAL

Low water on the Leek Arm & milepost at Consall

RUNNING through the upper valley of the Trent, a narrow, lacklustre stream difficult to equate with the river that this guide encounters at Derwentmouth, the Caldon Canal struggles to extricate itself from the urbanisation of The Potteries. Boaters have to cope with three lift-bridges: Ivy House (No.11) is electrified and has a fiendish reputation for being mechanically uncooperative; bridges 21 and 23 are hand-operated with a windlass. At MILTON a short arm once led to an ironworks and a colliery. "The Foxley", a friendly Ansells house, provides secure, offside customer moorings but there is no direct access for walkers. Milton provides a useful array of shops accessible from bridge 18. At Norton Green the Knypersley Feeder (long ago navigable to a remote colliery basin) joins the canal; Knypersley being one of three reservoirs, along with Stanley and Rudyard, which feed into the Caldon, and thence the Trent & Mersey, to maintain water levels. The fledging Trent is piped beneath the canal by bridge 22. A footpath leads to the scattered community of Norton Green and the mellifluently named "Foaming Quart Inn".

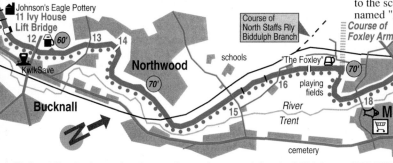

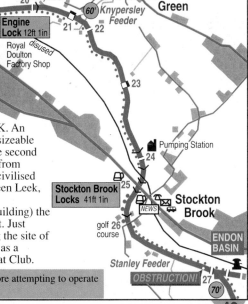

A flight of five locks carries the canal up to its summit level of 486 feet at STOCKTON BROOK. An attractive red brick water-board pumping station overlooks the bottom lock. There used to be a sizeable dock here for boats delivering coal. The old Stoke to Leek railway crosses the canal between the second and third locks. Disused now, but retained in case there is ever a resumption of the stone traffic from Cauldon Low, its rusty rails forlornly accompany much of the course of the Caldon Canal. In a civilised country with an integrated transport policy it would now be a rapid-transit interurban link between Leek, The Potteries and Newcastle-under-Lyne.

Beyond Stockton Brook (two cosy pubs and a newsagency housed in the old timber station building) the landscape of stone walls and small holdings begins to have a Pennine sense of obduracy about it. Just before bridge 27 an unusual circular metal platform obstructs the centre of the channel, marking the site of a light-railway swingbridge; boaters should steer carefully around this. Endon Basin, once used as a transhipment point for Cauldon Low limestone from rail to canal, is now occupied by Stoke Boat Club.

Ivy House Lift Bridge is operated with the use of a BW key. Make sure that the barriers are fully down before attempting to operate the bridge using the push button controls.

ARCING around Endon, the Caldon Canal heads for HAZELHURST JUNCTION. There is no more sublime a meeting or parting of waterways in the whole canal system. If, on arrival, you experience a sense of deja vu, then cast your mind back to Hardings Wood where the Macclesfield performs an equally acrobatic manoeuvre in departing the Trent & Mersey as the short Leek branch does the main line here. It wasn't always so. Originally the Caldon descended to the valley floor from Endon. Then, with construction of the Leek branch, the new line we use today was built, with a staircase lock forming an abrupt descent adjacent to bridge 3 at Denford. But the staircase was a bottleneck for the heavy traffic of limestone boats from Froghall, and so in 1841 the present layout was arrived at, with three single chambers taking

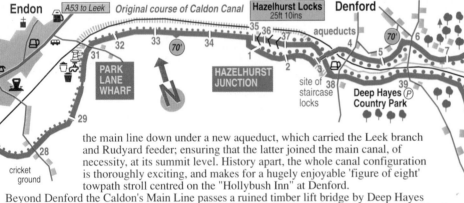

the main line down under a new aqueduct, which carried the Leek branch and Rudyard feeder; ensuring that the latter joined the main canal, of necessity, at its summit level. History apart, the whole canal configuration is thoroughly exciting, and makes for a hugely enjoyable 'figure of eight' towpath stroll centred on the "Hollybush Inn" at Denford.

Beyond Denford the Caldon's Main Line passes a ruined timber lift bridge by Deep Hayes Country Park where there are offside moorings for visiting boaters. Turning south-eastwards, the canal enters the Churnet Valley. Enclosed by high ridges, it reaches CHEDDLETON where a delightful flint mill, powered by twin waterwheels, graces the scene. In the past there were also limekilns, silk and paper mills and a brewery here. Again the canalscape is full of appeal. A restored Fellows, Morton & Clayton butty "Vienna" is moored by the mill. Built at Saltley, Birmingham in 1911 it had its name changed to "Verbena" during the First World War in case the mere sight of a name associated with "The Hun" would cause a riot. A plaque by Cheddleton top lock marks the re-opening of the Caldon Canal in 1974 after it had fallen into dereliction in the early 1960s. No one should pass this point without mouthing a silent 'thank you' to the waterway enthusiasts and local authorities who 'engineered' the canal's restoration.

*Figures refer to main line, allow 1 hour to cruise Leek Branch (one way).

A520 to Stone

The Leek Arm

From Hazelhurst, the branch to Leek curves away from the main line locking down to pass beneath it. Two overbridges preceed a sharp turn at the site of the old staircase locks before the branch crosses the main line on an imposing brick aqueduct dated 1841. A lesser aqueduct over the railway follows before the branch settles down on to the opposing hillside for its delightful journey towards Leek. Winding, dipping in and out of overbridges, and passing some envy-provoking waterside properties, the canal moves into a gorgeous belt of woodland where jays are to be heard screeching mockingly amongst the tree tops. In Spring these woods are full of bluebells. Presently the view ahead opens out towards the high flanks of The Morridge rising to 1,300ft in the east, whilst glowering over your right-hand shoulder stands the spooky tower of Leekbrook Asylum. If the inmates weren't deranged before they were incarcerated here, they would probably be sent mad by the sheer despondency of the hospital's grim institutional architecture.

All of a sudden the canal encounters a remote pool enclosed by low hills. The canal builders had no alternative but to dig a tunnel in order to reach Leek. The confined 130 yard bore is fronted by an ornate portal of red sandstone. Walkers take the horsepath across the top and are rewarded by stunning views over the town to the rocky pinnacles of The Roaches beyond.

Less than a mile of canal remains in water. The final turning point for all but the smallest cabin cruiser is just beyond bridge 9. Around the corner the canal peters out as its feeder comes in from Rudyard, three miles to the north. A public footpath (part of the "Staffordshire Way") follows the feeder to the reservoir which gave us the Kipling's christian name. An aqueduct, dated 1801, once carried the canal across the Churnet to reach a terminal wharf nearer the town centre. The aqueduct remains but is bereft of water, whilst the bed of the canal lies beneath an industrial estate. A sad loss to this now tourist-conscious town; though perhaps more could be done to enhance the setting of the current terminus.

Leek

A vigorous town of looming textile mills, gaunt Victorian architecture and some still cobbled streets, Leek is tucked away from the outside world in deep folds of the Staffordshire moorlands, conforming to everyone's mental image of a typical northern mill town. In fact it' is an entertaining and evocative place to explore, and canal travellers are entitled to mourn the disappearance of the old terminal arm and the resultant bleak trudge through an industrial estate which forms their initial, and definitely misleading, impression of Leek.

Eating & Drinking

PRIMO PIANO - Sheepmarket Street. Italian pizzeria/restaurant. Tel: 01538 398289.
GREYSTONES - Stockwell Street. Tearooms in 17th century house. Tel: 01538 398522.
JACQUELINES - Russell Street. Inexpensive yet atmospheric restaurant. Tel: 01538 381190.

Shopping

All facilities can be found in the town centre a mile north-east of the canal, though there is a large SAFEWAY store nearer at hand. The market is on Wednesday whilst Thursday is half-day. The chief charm of shopping in Leek lies in the adherence of many small shops to the old fashioned virtues of individuality and personal service. Each time we revisit the place to research a new edition we go 'heart in mouth' to St Edward's Street to make sure that PICKFORDS divine grocery store hasn't succumbed to late twentieth century trading patterns. Venerable advertisements for Ty-phoo, Bovril and Heinz (when they still had just 57 varieties) decorate the windows, whilst trays of fresh vegetables laid out on the pavement lure you in to be served by a gentleman in a white coat who glides from behind pyramids of tinned goods to await your every whim. More modern in outlook, but equally charming, is COUNTRY CUISINE in Sheepmarket Street, a friendly delicatessen and bakery. Don't go back to your boat without picking up some fresh oatcakes from ASPLINS on Haywood Street. Leek also boasts two secondhand bookshops together with several craft shops and art galleries. a number of the textile mills operate factory shops selling their products direct to the public.

Places to Visit

TOURIST INFORMATION CENTRE - Market Place. Tel: 01538 381000.
BRINDLEY MILL - Mill Street. Tel: 01538 399332. Open Easter- October Sat, Sun & BH Mons 2-5pm. Open same hours Mons, Tues & Weds in August. Restored water powered corn mill built by James Brindley in 1752. The museum illustrates millwrighting and much about the life of the great canal builder who spent his childhood in the town.

Public Transport

BUSES - frequent service to/from Hanley. Also connections with Cheddleton and Froghall vital to towpath walkers. Tel: 01782 747000.

BEYOND Cheddleton the enchantment deepens as the Caldon engenders an almost Amazonian sense of solitude. Briefly, in a distant echo of the arrangement at Alrewas (Map 16) the canal merges with the River Churnet at OAKMEADOW FORD LOCK, though there is little change of character, other than when heavy rainfall causes the river current to increase its normally sluggish pace.

You begin to wonder why on earth they ever bothered to build a canal in such an extraordinarily remote outpost of Staffordshire. But this is a countryside with plenty of skeletons in its closet. Haematite iron ore and limestone were extensively mined in the area, and there were also several coal shafts and flint-grinding mills. At its zenith in the 1860s, an average of thirty boats a day were carrying ore out of the Churnet Valley.

The Caldon Canal was promoted for two main reasons: for the export of limestone from Cauldon Low; and to provide the summit of the Trent & Mersey with extra water. It opened in 1779, but was literally the death of James Brindley, who caught a chill on a surveying trip, which turned to pneumonia and the subsequent demise of that genius of the early canal era.

Reaching CONSALL FORGE, the river disengages itself from the canal, disappearing over a weir to race ahead down the valley. The canal, however, makes light of this snub, passing under the railway, once a picturesque by-way of the North Staffordshire Railway, and now, some years after it was last used by sand trains, hopefully being brought back to life as a preserved steam line. The channel grows noticeably more slender, so that the passing of oncoming boats becomes a matter of discretion and a little 'give and take'. Squeezing past the cantilevered waiting room of Consall's old Beechinged station, the canal descends through the deep FLINT MILL LOCK, passes Consall Mill, and twists round the valley to the distinctively arched Cherry Eye bridge recalling, it is said, the inflamed, bloodshot eyes of the neighbourhood's ironstone workers.

A newly concreted section of canal follows as an embanked length prone to breaching is negotiated. Woodland tumbles down to the water's edge on one side, whilst on the other, an equally steep descent leads to the river. Suddenly a factory wall looms out of the trees, heralding the vast copper wire works of Thomas Bolton & Sons. The factory dates from 1890 and once operated a small fleet of narrowboats, though most of its transport needs were supplied by the railway. It was turned over to munitions during the war and apparently the Luftwaffe tried to bomb it but couldn't find it; not surprisingly when you take into account its position in this amphitheatre of hills.

Journey's end is frustratingly foreshortened for all but a few boaters by the restricted bore of FROGHALL TUNNEL. A sixty foot winding hole is provided by the copper works. If, however, your boat

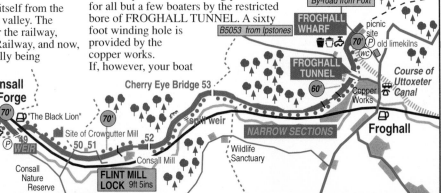

Froghall

conforms to within the tunnel's loading gauge displayed at Flint Mill Lock*, you can proceed to the picturesque terminal which lies beyond it. The rest of us must follow the path around the side.

Archive photographs of FROGHALL WHARF in its heyday have appeared in numerous publications, and it is hard to reconcile today's peace and quiet with the busy basin where limestone, brought down by plate tramway from the quarries, was cut to size and loaded on to narrowboats. The old scenes depict a conglomeration of sidings, great banks of limestone, smoking kilns, and, significantly, the top lock of the Uttoxeter extension, the site of which can still be discerned at the apex of the winding hole. But seventy odd years have passed since the wharf was abandoned commercially, and in the intervening period nature has reclaimed her own. a picnic site has been located in the shadow of the lime kilns and a tug-hauled trip-boat operates from the old wharf building. Three signposted walks can be enjoyed in the vicinity, or you can just laze by the canal, soaking in the setting's remarkable sense of calm and the fragility of time.

Cheddleton

(Map 42) Useful watering-hole before heading into the interior. The FLINTLOCK RESTAURANT offers "a wide variety of freshly prepared meals in relaxed and elegant surroundings"; bookings on 01538 361032. There are also three pubs in the village; closest to the canal, THE BOAT (bridge 44) is a snug little Marston's house. The post office stores by bridge 42 opens daily (am only on Sundays), whilst there's a small butcher's shop (closed Mondays) up the hill opposite the church.

Places to Visit

CHEDDLETON FLINT MILL - open weekend afternoons. One of the great little museums of England.
CHEDDLETON RAILWAY CENTRE - open Sundays and Bank Hols Easter - September. Short steam rides from the restored Pugin station. Hopes of extending along the Churnet Valley before much longer. Quaint refreshment rooms open daily (ex Thursdays) June to September. Tel: 01538 360522.

Public Transport

BUSES - services to/from Leek and Hanley useful for towpath walks. Tel: 01785 747000.

Consall Forge

Peace and tranquility characterise Consall to such an extent now that it is hard to visualise the activity of the forges, furnaces and slitting mills which clustered here in the seventeenth and eighteenth centuries. Now, though, it is for the isolated BLACK LION that Consall Forge is known. Ruddles, Worthington and Highgate mild are 'on tap' and the food is wholesome, inexpensive and served amidst a delightfully homely atmosphere, even when the landlady joins in with country & western on the radio. Just a stroll away is CONSALL NATURE PARK, its visitor centre open daily during the summer months.

Froghall

The 'village' consists almost entirely of the copper wire works, yet oddly enough this does not compromise the sense of isolation which pervades the otherwise unspoilt valley of the Churnet. The RAILWAY HOTEL is an Ind Coope pub offering bar lunches but there are no shops of any kind in Froghall. Buses offer a handy service for towpath walkers. Tel: 01782 747000. The trip boat operates public excursions on Thursday mornings and Sunday afternoons throughout the summer months. Tel: 01538 266486. A path leads from close to Cherry Eye Bridge to the WILDLIFE SANCTUARY open daily between 11am and 2.30pm. Tel: 01538 754784.

*Refer to page 71 for notes on navigating the Caldon Canal beyond Cheddleton.

Information

How to use the Maps

There are forty-three numbered maps. Maps 1 to 22 cover the Trent & Mersey Canal in its entirity from Preston Brook to Derwentmouth; Maps 13 and 23 to 27 cover the northern half of the Staffordshire & Worcestershire Canal; and Maps 27 to 40 cover the Shropshire Union from Autherley via Barbridge to Middlewich. The Caldon Canal, a branch of the Trent & Mersey, appears on Maps 8 and 41 to 43. Boaters navigating the FOUR COUNTIES RING should use Maps 4 to 13, and 27 to 40. Travelling clockwise around the ring - no matter where you start from - read the maps from left to right; anti-clockwise, right to left. For example, if you were to cruise the whole of the ring from Brewood in an anti-clockwise direction, you would turn first to Map 28 then 27, etc to 23; then 13, 12, 11 etc to 4; then 40, 39 etc back to 28. In any case the simplest way of proceeding from map to map is to turn to the next map numbered from the edge of the map you are on. Figures quoted at the top of each map refer to distance per map, locks per map and average cruising times. An alternative indication of timings from centre to centre can be found on the Route Planner inside the front cover. Obviously cruising times vary with the nature of your boat and the number of crew at your disposal, so quoted times should be taken only as an estimate. Neither do times quoted take into account any delays which might occur at lock flights in the high season.

Using the Text

Each map is accompanied by a route commentary describing the landscape and placing the canal in its historic context. Details of most settlements passed through are given together with itemised or summarised information of facilities likely to be of interest to canal users.

Eating & Drinking

Under this category we indicate a selection of establishments likely to be of use to users of the guide. We don't set out to make judgements in an Egon Ronay sense, but, generally speaking, the more detail we give, the more impressed we were with the place in question. It is desperately difficult to keep pace with changes at pubs and restaurants in particular, and we apologise in advance for any entries in the text subsequently overtaken by events.

Shopping

Shopping in strange towns and villages is one of the great pleasures of canal travel. Under this category we try to outline the basic facilities for shopping in any given location as well as mentioning any especially interesting, unusual, quirky, charming, or simply timeless shops worth patronising for the experience alone.

Places to Visit

This is the age of the 'one-third A4 tourist attraction leaflet' and you are doubtless already overloaded with bumph appertaining to every visitor centre within 50 miles radius of your itinerary. Nevertheless, we wouldn't be doing our job properly if we didn't outline attractions within easy reach of the canal, many of which seem all the more enjoyable when visited by boat.

Public Transport

Information in this category is quoted especially with the use of towpath walkers in mind, making 'one-way' walks using bus or train in the opposite direction. However we urge you to check with the telephone number quoted to ascertain up to the minute details of timetables etc.

Boating Facilities

Details of boat hire bases and boatyards offering facilities such as pumpout and fuel are quoted here. We no longer find it feasible to list every single service offered, but generally speaking the boatyards listed offer passing boaters all the services they are likely to require unless otherwise stated.

Walking

After years of official neglect and indifference, numerous towpath improvement schemes have reawakened public enthusiasm for walking beside canals. As an aid to walkers the maps in this guide depict the towpath in three categories: GOOD can usually be taken to indicate the existence of a firm, wide, dry base suitable for comfortable walking and cycling; ADEQUATE hints at the chance of mud and vegetation, but can usually be considered passable; whilst POOR speaks for itself - diehards may get through, but it won't be much fun. By and large the towing paths of the Four Counties Ring are in good condition. The worst stretches which spring to mind are between Stone and Great Haywood on the Trent & Mersey Canal; around Hatherton Junction on the Staffs & Worcs; and north of Audlem on the Shropshire Union. There are also some bad patches in the vicinity of Church Minshull on the Middlewich Branch.

Cycling

Cycling access to towpaths is an activity in its infancy, and British Waterways are only just beginning to come to terms with the concept of cycling for pleasure. To ride the towpaths you must first obtain a permit from any of the local Waterway Managers offices listed on page 71 or one or other of the Regional Offices covering the Four Counties Ring: British Waterways North West Region, Navigation Road, Northwich, Cheshire CW8 1BH. Tel: 01606 74321 or British Waterways, Midlands & South-West Region, Peel's Wharf, Fazeley, Tamworth, Staffs B78 3QZ. Tel: 01827 252000. With the permit will come a list of approved sections of towpath for cycling.

Boating

Boating virtually speaks for itself! We list all boatyards offering facilities to passers-by as well as all bases offering hire facilities and recommend you contact them direct for brochures and details of cost, availability etc.

Navigational Advice

Locks

Locks are part of the charm of canal cruising, but they are potentially dangerous environments for children, pets and careless adults. Use of them should be methodical and unhurried, whilst special care should be exercised in rain, frost and snow when slippery hazards abound. The locks on the FOUR COUNTIES RING and CALDON CANAL are of the familiar narrow-beam variety, but on the TRENT & MERSEY east of Burton-on-Trent they are wide beam and can fit two narrowboats side by side.

Moorings

Mooring on the canals featured in this guide is as per usual - ie on the towpath side, away from sharp bends, bridge-holes and narrows. Recommended moorings, of particular relevance to urban areas, are marked on the maps with an open bollard symbol. Long-term moorings, usually requiring a permit, are indicated with a closed bollard symbol. REMEMBER ALWAYS TO SLOW DOWN WHEN PASSING MOORED CRAFT.

Closures

Closures - known as 'stoppages' on the canals - usually occur between November and April when maintenance work is undertaken. Occasionally, however, an emergency stoppage may be imposed at short notice. Up to date details are usually available from hire bases. British Waterways provide a recorded message service for private boaters. The number to ring is: 01923 201401. Stoppages are also listed on pages 555 and 556 of Ceefax.

Harecastle Tunnel

A timetable of entry periods operates through the single-lane' tunnel at Harecastle on Map 7. In interests of safety the tunnel is only open when manned by the tunnel-keepers who have offices adjacent to the north and south portals of the tunnel. Current operating times are as follows:
WINTER HOURS - November to mid-March. The tunnel is closed except for booked passages. Telephone 0161 427 1079 giving at least 48 hours notice.

NORMAL HOURS - Mid March to mid May and mid September to end October. The tunnel is open for passage between 8am and 5pm. To be guaranteed a passage craft must arrive by 3pm.
SUMMER HOURS - Mid-May to Mid-September. As above but open until 6pm. For last guaranteed passage arrive by 4pm.

Caldon Canal

Beyond Cheddleton the Caldon Canal merges briefly with the River Churnet. At Oakmeadowford Lock a gauge indicates water safety levels and boaters are advised not to enter the river if the water level is over the six inch mark. Froghall Tunnel is extremely restricted in width and height and most boats are unlikely to be able to squeeze through; a notice board at Flint Mill Lock shows the dimensions you should adhere to. A 60 feet long winding hole exists by the Copper Works on the Hazelhurst side of the tunnel, but if your boat is a seventy-footer you are advised to turn at the last full length turning point above Flint Mill Lock. If you are able to pass through the tunnel a full length winding hole is located at Froghall Wharf.

Preston Brook Tunnel

At weekends and Bank Holidays between April and October, entry to the tunnel is subject to a timetable of segregated northbound and southbound hour long periods. These are:
Northbound 9-10, 12-13, 15-16, 18-19 and 21-22.
Southbound 7.30-8.30, 10.30-11.30, 13.30-14.30, 16.30-17.30 and 19.30-20.30. At other times do not enter the tunnel if a boat is already approaching from the opposite direction.

Acknowledgements

Thanks: to Steve Wicks of the Portfolio Press who took us through the quantum jump to computerisation; to all at Alvechurch Boat Centres for organising the research boat.; to ace researchers Les & Wendy Robinson; and to all our correspondents who keep us on the straight and narrow. Brian Collings's front cover design is in homage to Glasgow's trams!

Useful Contacts

Waterway Managers are responsible for individual sections of canal. The offices relevant to the canals covered by this guide are as follows:

BRITISH WATERWAYS
Church Lane
Marple
SK6 6BN
Tel: 0161 427 1079
(T&M north of Trentham
& Caldon Canal)

BRITISH WATERWAYS
Fradley Junction
Burton-on-Trent
DE13 7DN
Tel: 01283 790236
(T&M south of Colwich)

BRITISH WATERWAYS
Norbury Junction
Stafford
ST20 0PN
Tel: 01785 284253
(Staffs & Worcs, T&M
Trentham to Colwich and
Shropshire Union
south of Audlem)

BRITISH WATERWAYS
Birch Road
Ellesmere
Shropshire
SY12 9AA
Tel: 01691 622549
(SUC north of Audlem
inc Middlewich Arm)

Outside office hours, BW operate a central emergency telephone service. Dial the operator and ask for FREEPHONE CANALS. For mobile phone users the number is 01384 240948.

We are well known in the region
for our fine, authentic, traditional
style narrow boats . . .

"MAPLE' AT TYRLEY
Photo: Courtesy Robin Nicholson

. . . but did you know that we also hire
comfortable 'cruiser' and 'semi-trad' style boats?

4-12 BERTH, ECONOMY GRADE TO LUXURY,
SITUATED AT PROBABLY THE MOST STRATEGIC
LOCATION NORTH OF BIRMINGHAM!
for brochure contact:

MIDDLEWICH NARROWBOATS
35 CANAL TERRACE
MIDDLEWICH, CHESHIRE CW10 9BD
Telephone: Middlewich (01606) 832460